IT'S ALL IN THE KNOWING

IT'S ALL IN THE KNOWING

BISHOP J. A. TOLBERT 1ST

authorHOUSE®

AuthorHouse™
1663 Liberty Drive
Bloomington, IN 47403
www.authorhouse.com
Phone: 1-800-839-8640

Published by AuthorHouse   01/16/2013

ISBN: 978-1-4772-7724-9 (sc)
ISBN: 978-1-4772-7723-2 (hc)
ISBN: 978-1-4772-7711-9 (e)

Library of Congress Control Number: 2012919093

TABLE OF CONTENTS

Dedication ix
Preface xi

Chapter 1   It's All in the Knowing 1
Chapter 2   The Anatomy of a "Knowing"—The Power
             of Revelation 4
Chapter 3   The Cost of Knowing—the Cost of the Walk 12
Chapter 4   One Moment of "Knowing vs. Twelve
             Years of Logic 16
Chapter 5   The Purpose of the "Knowing" 23
Chapter 6   God and His gods KNOW! 27
Chapter 7   In God but Not In Christ 32
Chapter 8   Are you in the Spirit or of the Flesh? 44
Chapter 9   Take it all off—Put it all ON! 54
Chapter 10   Can you Really Afford the "Old Man?" 70
Chapter 11   Potentials of the "Old Man" vs. Potentials
             of the "New Man" 73
Chapter 12   A Surprise Worth Waiting For! 81
Chapter 13   Put Off, Renew and Put On! 86
Chapter 14   To Renew is to "Re-Know" 93
Chapter 15   The "Best" is in The Knowing! 100
Chapter 16   Patience Power 108
Chapter 17   Hope is in the "Knowing!" 112
Chapter 18   Prudence and Wisdom vs. Faith 115

Chapter 19   The Faith Equation.....................................118
Chapter 20   Heaven's Word—the Final Answer.................121
Chapter 21   Faith Full Ones do Not Stagger 124
Chapter 22   Four Forms of Belief..................................128
Chapter 23   Faith's Litmus Test 136
Chapter 24   What's Missing? "Greater Works!".................138
Chapter 25   A "Game" God Plays 143
Chapter 26   Perfect Imperfection? 147
Chapter 27   God Promised? 150
Chapter 28   Less Truly Is More! 156
Chapter 29   Perfect Love Inspires Radical Love 162
Chapter 30   The Five Looks 168
Chapter 31   The Three-fold Plan....................................177
Chapter 32   Doubt, the Heart Problem—Faith, the
             Heart Solution...182
Chapter 33   Death's Great Disdainer 185
Chapter 34   The Great Complainer 187
Chapter 35   It Wasn't Me or Was IT? 192
Chapter 36   The Battle of the Wars 197
Chapter 37   From Complainer to Conqueror....................200
Chapter 38   Do you Really Know You?.............................210
Chapter 39   Moved by the Hand of God 219
Chapter 40   Bones Too Dead, Bones Too Dry 224
Chapter 41   It's Still in The Knowing 228
Chapter 42   Prophesy for All Who Have no
             Voice—Believe for all Who Have no Heart.........231
Chapter 43   Breathing His Breath 234
Chapter 44   "I Will do" and "Ye Shall Know!"....................237
Chapter 45   Confusion Precedes Order and Clarity.............242
Chapter 46   Dead To Live..247
Chapter 47   Preaching: The Breath of Life 250
Chapter 48   Hallelujah-tosis: The Breath
             of a Second Chance 254

Chapter 49   What They Know is What They "Say" and
              What They "Say" is What They Get! 257
Chapter 50   The Great "Gravebreak" 260
Chapter 51   The Great Great Gravebreak 265
Chapter 52   Dead and Refusing to Die! 267
Chapter 53   The Value of a Torn Veil......................................270
Chapter 54   You Must Know Who and What You Are 279
Chapter 55   Faith is About Giving God a Name 282
Chapter 56   It's Still All in The Knowing! 285
Chapter 57   What We Fought With, Denied For and
              Stood On..289
Chapter 58   "His "Name" is More Than the word,
              "Jesus!" Know that!" 297

Epilogue 305
About the Author..311

DEDICATION

This book is dedicated to my "Brown Sugar," my Rosemary. Having been married to her now for forty-seven years, I can truly say that I have loved my childhood sweetheart for almost my entire life. I thank you, "Sally" for your love and for believing in me and seeing something worthy in me that sometimes I didn't see in myself.

This book is also dedicated to John 2nd (John-John), Kai, Rosemarie, ("RohMahree") Lamar Terrill, Shawn Aric, Lacy and Shawneen Marie ("Nee-Nee") and LaVell, (who I have not given up on) my wonderful and gifted children whom I love more than words can describe.

My sixteen Grandchildren most certainly put the "Grand" in Grandchildren. To you I write this book and pray that one day you will find in its pages a path to God and your potentials in Him and follow that Way all the days of your life in the comfort and safety of His Love with a real certainty and expectation of living with Jesus forever.

To my Church family that I have been privileged to pastor since September 6, 1976, I have written this book. My heart is filled with profound gratitude for your love, your devotion the stage of our lives! I knew that all the years of teaching and preaching that we had received from some of Zion's most anointed and biblically accurate teachers of our day had prepared these stalwart warriors of the Faith for these Revelations; for these lessons; for these days.

Nevertheless, some of my life's greatest frustrations were realized as the excitement and elation of my congregants seemed to wane and diminish after the teachings were ended and life's business called the Saints attention. At the realization of this exceptionally negative phenomenon, I began to plead, beg and even verbally coerce my Church family to study their notes, reread the printed material and get copies of the DVDs and CDs that I worked so hard to produce and put into their hands. But much to my dismay, these overtures seemed to be ignored having fallen on, *seemingly,* deaf ears. I even had the lessons taught by other teachers in the church but the lessons these oracles taught had no greater effect than my teaching had! The teachers did endeavor to repeat the passion with which I had taught the lesson. They tried to be as excited about the truths as I had been—but to no avail!

My distress was enormous! My heart's regret was almost tangible! What had happened? Where were the benefits of these hours upon hours of praying, studying and writing! Eventually, the same elated response that the people had to these lessons that had previously gave me such exquisite joy became hollow and unfulfilling sounds of wasted opportunities! Gone was singing in my heart! Gone was the pride in the spiritual astuteness and scriptural preparedness of my flock! It even seemed that the ministries of the late Elder Samuel D. Tolbert Sr., the late Bishop Horace M.

Young, Bishop Noel Jones, Bishop Richard Young, Elder Winfred Garrett, Bishop Daryl Shaw and Bishop Grace had somehow lost their effectiveness!

I labored much in both prayer and deep cogitation over this matter. I pondered what I thought was "Satan's latest attack on our Church" and finally **another "*Knowing*"** was conceived in my spirit! God began to speak to me gently and lovingly as only He can.

He reminded me that often **His personal teachings were ignored, rejected and misunderstood. "From that *time* many of his disciples went back, and walked no more with him."** (Joh 6:66) The "icing on the cake" though, was Jesus' reminder that when He asked Peter "... **But whom say ye that I am?" And Simon Peter answered and said, Thou art the Christ, the Son of the living God. And Jesus answered and said unto him, Blessed art thou, Simon Barjona: for flesh and blood hath not revealed *it* unto thee, but my Father which is in heaven.** (Mat 16:25-17)

It must be noted that Jesus gave reason for Peter's answer. He would not allow Peter or the rest of the disciples to imagine that Peter was so clever, so smart and intelligent that he could *by means of his own understanding* identify the Son of God. This Revelation; *this Knowing **had to be endowed by the Father!***

Similarly, all who would be recipients of the truths that herein lie must seek God for a Revelation and a ***Knowing!*** **"But the natural man receiveth not the things of the Spirit of God: for they are foolishness unto him:**

neither can he know *them,* **because they are spiritually discerned.**" (1Co 2:14)

Just as I was seeking Revelatory knowledge when God gave me these *Knowings* and just as the revelation of Who Jesus is was revealed to Peter, so must my congregation apply themselves as must you, Dear Reader, apply yourself to seeking the anointing that will transfigure the truths of this book into a life changing Revelation; into a transforming—*Knowing!*

If the reader does not respect these truths enough to seek God by lying before Him and waiting in faith believing for *the Knowing* that **is God's Gift of His Mind in us**—the reader will simply read a book! But if the reader will seek God and allow Him to create in the reader Divine Understanding, this book will become a source of Life and Miracles such as the reader has never experienced before!

(Interspersed between some of the chapters the reader will find excerpts from a book that that I have written called, "Feathers from the Eagle's Wings." The book is chock full of golden nuggets of spiritual wisdom that the Lord gave me at various times in my life! One nugget I received from my father, the late Elder Samuel D. Tolbert Sr.

CHAPTER 1

IT'S ALL IN THE KNOWING

A Key Question for This Chapter

*"What is the "**Knowing**" that converts idiocy and lunacy into noble courage as men fight "unbeatable foes" and go "where the brave dare not go?"*

Depression, fear, heartbreak and pain are not strangers to most of us. Stressed related diseases account for more sicknesses and deaths than in other cause in America today. In Luke 21:26, Jesus speaks of **"Men's hearts failing them for fear . . . ."** The words of the late President Franklin D. Roosevelt seem to "fall on deaf ears" today! His First Inaugural Address which was spoken in1932 was marked with these words, *"So, first of all, let me assert my firm belief that **the only thing we have to fear is fear itself**—nameless, unreasoning, unjustified terror which paralyzes needed efforts to convert retreat into advance."* He knew that if fear or any other debilitating weakness of character was to run unchecked among the nation, America would retreat and

1

the loss to her would change life in America as they knew it in that day—*forever!*

Our nemesis, Satan, also knows with even greater clarity then the wisest man on earth the consequences of the Church giving ground and losing the battle for the Kingdom of God to the hordes of Hell. So, the gauntlet is thrown! The challenge has been given and accepted! The battle is on! The great problem is that the battleground is the arena of the human mind and spirit! Though the trophies so hard fought for are often material and in equal measure, intangible, Satan's most sought after prizes are the relationship between God and man and ultimately—the souls of man! He well knows the emotional attachment mankind has with his earthly treasures be they "... **of the flesh ... of the eyes** ... or of **the pride of life.**" (1 John 2:16)

It is a fact that the Saints of the Most High God are marked for persecution, tribulation and death. The writer of the epistle to the Hebrews observes, **"Ye have not yet resisted unto blood, striving against sin."** (Heb. 12:4) The small but key word, *"yet"* <u>is of prime importance</u> for it speaks both of things past and things still to come! The understanding here is that ***up to this moment*** you have not resisted unto blood <u>striving against sin</u>! But the very clear implication is *the day is sure to come* when you shall taste your own blood and see it spilled for the name of Christ! The moment will arrive when you will be faced with the fateful decision to deny God and live or affirm him and die!

"Ye have not yet resisted unto blood, striving against sin." The prophet, Jeremiah, very thoughtfully and with great insight, wonders and asks Israel, **"If thou hast run with the footmen, and they have wearied thee, then how canst thou contend with horses?"** (Jer.12:5) The question begs to be asked, "If you couldn't *handle the adversities that did not threaten your life—how will you survive the temptations in which both* **excruciating pain and death may result?**

Thus, one may wonder, "How can anyone suffer the pain, the mental anguish and the fear of resisting **"unto blood"** and emerge victorious? What is it that must be **known** to cause one to struggle against seemingly impossible odds? What is the strength whereby reasonably thinking people dream to do unachievable deeds and strive to attain virtually unattainable goals? And, is it madness to harbor in the heart a hope that ever "springs eternal?" What is the *"Knowing"* that converts idiocy and lunacy into noble courage as men fight "unbeatable foes" and "go where the brave dare not go!" It is to this end that this book is written.

CHAPTER 2

——⊰◆⊱——

THE ANATOMY OF A
"KNOWING"—THE POWER
OF REVELATION

The Key Phrase of this Chapter

*". . . the crowning touch to growth is development or
"becoming" and **"becoming"** is the direct result of a
"knowing" at work!"*

For the benefit of this treatise <u>**"The Knowing"** is
synonymous with **"The Revelation."**</u>

The active ingredients of the mental process: thinking,
learning, and knowledge do have value in their own rights.
But they become infinitely more powerful and far reaching
in their effects when they are blended with the divine
catalyst—*"a Knowing" (a Revelation)!* A *Knowing* is truly
a "motivational understanding!" God's desire is that you
learn but not just so that you *may know*, rather, that you
may become something you have never been and to become

that more fully; more perfectly than you have ever known was possible. While many people who revere knowledge hang their hats on learning and growing as the ends all of maturity, God has revealed to me that *the crowning touch to growth is development* or **"becoming"** and **"becoming"** is the direct result of a *knowing* at work!

Some astute scholar of life has observed that *"often better_is the enemy of best."* There are those people who will be satisfied to simply improve and will defend their acts by pointing out that "At least I am not as bad as I used to be!" They have not gotten it right but they can see progress and that is good enough for them! Contessa

Similarly, many times, *knowledge and logic are enemies of Knowing and revelation!* Because they are satisfied with their understanding of an issue, many people don't seek a revelation (*a Knowing*) and are thereby left with the mediocre and the average when they could have accomplished the splendid and the magnificent that only divine *"Knowing"* can provide!

Knowledge only gives information—*"Knowing and revelation"* cause transformation and manifestation. To reiterate, information can produce knowledge but *a Knowing produce s a transformation and a manifestation!* Any truth that does not change you has not become a Knowing in your heart! The Knowing has a life and a power of its own! Words of The Knowing are anointed; infused with the Presence of God! Surely, as Jesus said with copious clarity, **". . . the words I speak unto you, they are spirit, and they are life!"** (Joh.6:63b) The words of *The Knowing* do not only **have** spirit—*they are spirit!* **The**

5

<u>**words of The Knowing do not only have life—they _are_ life inducing!**</u>

For the word of God _is_ quick . . . . (Heb 4:12)

1. The **"Word,"** God, is presented in three different forms. There is the Essential "Word," _God Himself_ Who is ". . . **The Almighty God, The Everlasting Father and The Prince of Peace."** (Isa. 9:6)

   a. The **Essential** **"Word"** is (among other things) known as the "**Alpha and Omega, the beginning and the ending, saith the Lord, which is, and which was, and which is to come."** (Rev 1:8)

      i. The **Essential "Word"** is the Creator Who spoke His Eternal and Infallible Word and said, **"Let there be . . . ."** (Gen. 1:3 and 6)

      ii. The **Essential "Word"** caused His Spoken **"Word"** to go out from Himself _without leaving Himself_ (because there was absolutely _no place for His Word to go **but in Himself**)!_

      iii. So, His **"Word"** went _out from Him_ and _into Him without leaving Him_ and _became the epitome and the personification of His Divine Thought: earth, water, sun moon and stars etc.!_

b. Then there is the **Written "Word,"** meaning *the Holy Scriptures.*

    i. Consider 2nd Peter 1:21, **"For the prophecy came not in old time by the will of man: but holy men of God spake *as they were moved by the Holy Ghost.*"** (2Pe 1:21)

    ii. The **Essential "Word"** of God, by the agency, authority and Power of His Regenerative Word—inspired men *both by writing His Word and by audibly speaking* His Word to communicate His Word and His Will to His people."

c. The Regenerative "Word" of God is (in a word) "Christ!"

    i. So it is that Christ Jesus is the Element in the nature of the **Essential "Word"** of God that is responsible *for the divinely indwelt individual* being able to hear the "Words" of the **Regenerative "Word"** of God. Note Rom. 10:17, **". . . faith *cometh* by hearing, and hearing by the word of God."** (

    ii. The **Regenerative "Word"** of God is the aspect of the **Essential "Word"** that is the quality of His Omniscience, Omnipotence and His Omnipresence that creates the sinner anew by indwelling the sinner and empowering by living righteously and godly through the surrendered life.

7

    iii. The **Regenerative "Word"** lives a Holy Lifestyle in the surrendered life.

    iv. The **Regenerative "Word"** also lives *as a god on earth **through the life of the surrendered soul.***

d. Then there is the **Spoken "Word,"** *the Word that God uttered.*

    i. Whenever God speaks—He changes something! Nothing that the **Spoken "Word"** of God says **leaves the world just as it was before God spoke!**

    ii. For when He speaks

        1. Laws are decreed!
        2. The natural has been touched by the Supernatural!
        3. Something is built up, torn down or protected from any change!
        4. Deliverance is bestowed or devastation is wrought!
        5. Peace is imparted or war is declared!
        6. Life is given or life is forfeited!
        7. But something is inexorably changed (to use a legal term) **"with prejudice!"**

    iii. The worlds were not made from things that were visible or tangible but *by the Infallible "Word" of God.*

iv. **Through faith we understand that the worlds were framed by the word of God, so that things which are seen <u>were not made of things which do appear.</u>** (Heb. 11:3)

e. The Spoken "Word" is that Authority that spangled the night with stars and set the sun blazing in the heavens.

That SpokenWord **is quick!** (See Heb. 4:12) The word "quick" is from the Greek word, "zao" that means *"alive"* and *"live"* and *"quick."* (Strong's #G2198) So, the word of God is not only life that causes things to come into existence and causes existing things to live, it also causes those things that are dead to come back to life! Thus, the Living Word effects what never was; what is and what used to be! ***Knowing this truth*** (having a revelation concerning this truth) places the most real and profound hope of resurrection in the deepest echelons of the believer's being!

Remember, Dear Student, Jesus said, "... **the truth** ..." (John 8:32) **(The Knowing**; the revelation) "... **<u>shall make you</u> free!" But only the truth** (The Knowing; the revelation) **<u>that you know!</u>** The power of Truth is frustrated and rendered null and void in the heart of the soul that is ignorant of truth! **How then shall they call on him in whom they have not believed? and how shall they believe in him of whom they have not heard? (Rom 10:14)** If they don't know the truth they shall remain in bondage!

9

"... **shall make you free!**" By Divine ordination, Truth should not merely *be*—it should *live; it should make you; it should effect change* and *it should influence*! In other words, **The Knowing will cause you to "become"** because *The Knowing is possessive!* It has a life of its own and if left uninterrupted and to its own agenda—it will work the works of the Lord in our lives!

(Isa 55:9)**For *as* the heavens are higher than the earth, so are my ways higher than your ways, and my thoughts than your thoughts.**

A "***Knowing***" is *a Divine Thought* and **a *Way*** that is so Heavenly and so much higher than man's thoughts and man's ways of doing things that God has to uniquely and singularly reveal the ***Thought*** and the ***Way*** **to the mind** *that God has prepared to receive it.* To perhaps make the "***Knowing***" more easily understood, a "***Knowing***" is a "Revelatory Word of God;"

- a "Word of God" that has its origin in the Heart of God
- a "Word of God" that reveals the essence of both the intent and the spirit of God's perfect Will
- a "Word of God" that He prepares man to receive; a "Word of God" that He expresses to man;
- a "Word of God" that He clarifies to man; a "Word of God" that is received by man and
- a "Word of God" that should be (by man) *given free rein in the heart of man.*

As long as Truth lives in obscurity and ambiguity and as long as Divine Reality is hidden in confusion and perplexity—**THERE IS NO *KNOWING!* THERE**

IS NO REVELATION! THERE IS NO KNOWN TRUTH! And until the Light of Veracity is revealed and the facts have been freed from behind the veneer of enigma, secrecy and mystery—**THERE IS NO *KNOWING!***

CHAPTER 3

THE COST OF *KNOWING*—THE COST OF THE WALK

The Key Phrase of this Chapter

"And the price paid is usually equal to the value of the knowledge gained!"

It has been said that the best knowledge is "bought" knowledge! In other words, there is always a price that is paid for knowledge! And the price paid is usually equal to the value of the knowledge gained! Information, however, is usually more cheaply received than knowledge. Quite often, information is freely given while knowledge is often obtained either from one "going through hard trials" with God or enduring the harsh realities of life in this earth realm. Suffice it to say that "*Knowing*" may be acquired at a premium cost!

Heb. 10:32 But call to remembrance the former days, in which, after ye were illuminated, ye endured a great fight of afflictions;

Pointing church members to their life before their redemption, the Lord admonishes them to remember when ". . . **after ye were illuminated . . . ,**" God **"called you out of darkness into his marvelous light . . . ." (1 Pet.2:9 KJV)** He wanted them to remember how they bore great hardship and endured intolerable things while they suffered unmentionable loss. It was then that they learned that although salvation is free *you will pay a great price to get to Heaven!* It will cost everything; your identity; your own aspirations; your finances and all of your treasures! All must be either **given up _for God_** or **given over _to God_** if one would walk with the King!"

33 Partly, whilst ye were made a gazingstock both by reproaches and afflictions; and partly, whilst ye became companions of them that were so used.

Now hear God speaking through the writer's heart saying, "You knew some of your misery and distress while you were being gawked at because you were suffering the reproaches and afflictions of vile men who *"speak evil of dignities." (See Jude 1:8b)* You also became a spectacle by being verbally and physically attacked and you had to live under constraints that were far beneath what you believed was reasonable. Other of your turmoil was lived as you joined yourself to the plight and the suffering of your spiritual yokefellows." Throughout scripture it can be seen that you are in very good company who are so minded to do the same. Note Moses' example, **"By faith Moses, when he was come to years, refused to be called the son of Pharaoh's daughter; Choosing rather to suffer affliction with the people of God, than to enjoy the pleasures of sin for a season; Esteeming the reproach of Christ**

13

greater riches than the treasures in Egypt: for he had respect unto the recompence of the reward. By faith he forsook Egypt, not fearing the wrath of the king: for he endured, as seeing him who is invisible. Through faith he kept the passover, and the sprinkling of blood, lest he that destroyed the firstborn should touch them." (Heb 11:24-28)

Now, please consider Heb. 10:34 **"For ye had compassion of me in my bonds, and took joyfully the spoiling of your goods, *knowing* in yourselves that ye have in heaven a better and an enduring substance."**

The learned apostle to the Jews, is asserting here, "You cared, sympathized and knew a godly pride in me for the stand I took in times of horrific personal sacrifice for the Gospel. Bolstered and supported by my example, you cheerfully and with much bliss accepted the ruination of your treasures. You were fortified by the assurances and the certainties of a glorious eternity with our Savior and His Saints. You were more than willing to make the trade of temporal treasures on earth for *the prizes of wealth and riches in Heaven where no depreciation or erosion can affect their worth.* For the immeasurable joy and the exquisite delight of finally basking in His Eternal Presence, you gleefully and with many praises took the "wrong for the right!" And while suffering indignities that were the measure of man's inhumanity to man—you **walked purposefully and boldly into the fires of adversity.**

Everything man knows is the result of man having an experience. The difference between knowing and conjecturing is that a *"Knowing"* is backed up and bolstered by evidence while conjecture is simply hypothesis that is the product of an educated or uneducated *guess.* A "*Knowing*" will usually reside in that part of the brain that houses realities and the "guess" is found in the part of the brain where imagination and fantasies are held.

These noble acts of self-sacrifice, uncommon courage and devotion were lived because, as Paul said of the Hebrew Church, "You had a "*knowing* <u>in yourselves . . . .</u>" Their *knowing* was in the deepest echelons of their being! They were not vacillating or halted between two opinions. (See1ˢᵗ Kings 18:21) The "die was cast;" "the jury was in" and "the votes were counted in each heart!" They had a "*motivating understanding*" about this truth!

CHAPTER 4

ONE MOMENT OF "KNOWING VS. TWELVE YEARS OF LOGIC

The Key Truth in this Chapter

*"Both her ignorance and her **Knowing** compelled her to come"*

Mar 5:25 **And a certain woman, which had an issue of blood twelve years,**

Mar 5:26 **And had suffered many things of many physicians, and had spent all that she had, and was nothing bettered, but rather grew worse,**

Mar 5:27 **When she had heard of Jesus, came in the press behind, and touched his garment.**

Mar 5:28 **For she said, If I may touch but his clothes, I shall be whole.**

Mar 5:29 **And straightway the fountain of her blood was dried up; and she felt in** *her* **body that she was healed of that plague.**

Mar 5:30 **And Jesus, immediately knowing in himself that virtue had gone out of him, turned him about in the press, and said, Who touched my clothes?**

Mar 5:31 **And his disciples said unto him, Thou seest the multitude thronging thee, and sayest thou, Who touched me?**

Consider, now, the woman that the Apostle, Mark, brings to our attention here. First of all, we may know that this rehearses an episode in the life of Jesus because Mark starts his testimony with an acknowledgement that this is concerning **"a <u>certain</u> woman."** This is a narrative of a real life episode in Jesus' life and not a parable that is written simply to illustrate a point of knowledge. This really happened!

Secondly, note that this woman had been suffering with a hemorrhage for twelve long years and had endured at the hands of many physicians and their inadequate medical knowledge. The tragic result was both physical and financial for she **"had spent all that she had, and was nothing bettered, but rather grew worse!"**

It is so wonderful when we find those very special people who have decided in their heart that *"I am not going out like this!"* These may not know just what the remedy is or the cost of it but they are more than willing to be healed—they are determined to be healed! They may not know the "hows," the "whys" or the "whos" of their deliverance—*but they know that* **they must and they shall—**<u>**be healed!**</u>

In this case of an astounding miracle being done in an individual's life, the phenomenon occurred because of what the woman **did not know** as much as what she **did know!** As aforementioned, ***she did not know*** how, why, who or where concerning her healing. But ***she knew*** that she had to be healed! ***She knew*** she was not destined to live the rest of her life in this deplorable state. ***She was certain*** that she was **NOT** going to die because of this condition! It was because of *her resolve to live* **and** because she did not know *how she was going to stay alive* that, **"W hen she had heard of Jesus . . ,"** she **". . . <u>came in the press behind, and touched</u>** his garment. **(**Mar 5:27) Both her ignorance and her ***Knowing*** compelled her to come very close to breaking with Jewish tradition and Jewish law when she put her hands on a man's clothes Whom she did not know and (*the worse thing was her timing*) while she was in her "unclean" (the issue of blood) condition! (See Lev. 15:19-20)

It not known whether the woman who is the focus of this miracle ever heard Jesus say, **". . . <u>whosoever shall say</u> unto this mountain, Be thou removed, and be thou cast into the sea; <u>and shall not doubt in his heart</u>, but <u>shall believe</u> that those things which he saith shall come to pass; <u>he shall have whatsoever he saith.</u>** (Mar 11:23) However, we do know that, though our Lord is no respecter of persons, He is a respecter of principles! So, when **". . . she said, If I may touch but his clothes, I shall be whole"** (Mar 5:28) **she activated those elements in**

Jesus that cause Him to trigger His healing powers. Those catalysts were:

❖ her knowing,
❖ her faith,
❖ her need and
❖ her actions that were her response to her *Knowing*; her faith and her need.

For she said, If I may touch but his clothes, I shall be whole. (Mar 5:28)

By the time the woman touched the hem of Jesus' garment she was no longer in control of herself! Her *Knowing* had completely taken over her mind and body! Note Mark's testimony! **When she had heard of Jesus, came in the press behind, and touched his garment.** (Mar 5:27) <u>**For she said,**</u> **If I may touch but his clothes, I shall be whole."** (Mar 5:28) She **"touched"** because **"<u>she said!"</u>** And *she said—because she Knew!*

To be succinct and transparently clear,

❖ *She heard of Jesus* (hope lived and *The Knowing* was born)
❖ *She came to Jesus* (*The Knowing* compelled her)
❖ *She touched Jesus* (faith came into contact with Power and Love)
❖ *She was healed* (the transformation was complete and the manifestation occurred)

Mar 5:29 **And straightway the fountain of her blood was dried up; and she felt in** *her* **body that she was healed of that plague.**

Faith works! Though the answer or the deliverance may not **appear** immediately it is a done deal as soon as *The Knowing* and faith galvanize the power of God into action! In this case, the remedy was **"straightway"** meaning **"immediate!"** Remember, Precious Heart, that I told you that a "Revelation and a *Knowing* produce a transformation and a manifestation!" The confirmation is right here! It is because the woman had a *Knowing* that—she acted! Because <u>she acted</u>—**God acted!** When <u>God acted</u>—*she was transformed!* The manifestation was evident! **". . . She felt in** *her* **body that she was healed of that plague."** (Mar 5:29) The body must prove and confirm with evidence the truth of the spirit of your mind! So, ". . . **straightway the fountain of her blood was dried up; she <u>felt in</u> <u>her</u> <u>body</u> that she was healed of that plague."** And she **was healed!** It was the positive effects of the healing that confirmed to the flesh that she had a true *Knowing!* Her healing was a fact in her heart before her blood ever dried up! Don't forget that she declared within herself, ". . . **If I may touch but his clothes, I shall be whole."** (Mar 5:28) *The Knowing will produce an undeniable transformation which will bring to pass a permanent manifestation and a demonstration of the miracle!* The manifestation may not appear in tangible and visible form right away but faith is, after all, ". . . **the substance of things hoped for, the evidence of things not seen."**(Heb. 1:1) Consequently, after she surrendered to the possessiveness and the control of *The Knowing*—it was simply a matter of time before the work of *The Knowing* (Divine agenda) was done!

Mar 5:30 **And Jesus, immediately knowing in himself that virtue had gone out of him, turned him about in the press, and said, Who touched my clothes?**

Though the woman touched *the hem of Jesus' garment*, *The Knowing* (the Mind of God) had a more direct target to aim for—**the very Heart of the Son of God!** *The Knowing* cannot be denied access to anything or anybody! When the woman touched the hem of His garment in faith believing and in response to her need, *The Knowing* stimulated the healing virtue of our Lord. When He felt the virtue leave Him, Jesus knew that healing virtue had gone from Him to answer the call of faith! His only concern was to know who had been blessed to receive *The Knowing* that loosed the faith that called on His healing virtue. You must understand that this woman's healing that day was not a new thing in the heart of God! God had this planned even before the foundation of the world! The ultimate purpose of *The Knowing* is to effect the changes *in our lives* that are God's Perfect Will *for our Lives!*

Those who "**. . . had compassion of . . .**" Paul "**. . . in his bonds, and took joyfully the spoiling of . . .**" their "**. . . goods,** had a *Knowing* that they stood on and if that posture was a gamble—they bet it all on the truth that they "**. . . have in heaven a better and an enduring substance.**" The woman with the issue of blood had her *Knowing* also! They all possessed and were possessed by a *Knowing* that transcended and overcame every logic, cost of suffering and temptation! For, that is the strength of a true *Knowing!* It takes control and is a governing force that raises itself in opposition to all and everything that opposes it and—IT WINS!

A Feather from the Eagle's Wing

Warrantees come with automobiles and toasters—guarantees only come with the Will of God!

CHAPTER 5

THE PURPOSE OF THE "*KNOWING*"

A Key Definition for this Chapter

*The power of a "**knowing**" is that it produces thoughts that produce actions that produce habits that become, determine and define our character in God!*

The grand purpose for gaining knowledge is that the opportunity to change will be provided. Gaining knowledge simply for the purpose of having information is an exercise in futility! To change just for the purpose of doing something different is really a waste of time! *You should change for the purpose of **becoming**!*

Among other things, God wants me to *inspire you to think* but more than that—to *"re-think!"* Re-think so as to see anew those wonders of spiritually enlivened imagination that ignite sparks of joys of new potentials. Also re-thinking gives new life to old promises and possibilities! Additionally, proper re-thinking clarifies, fine tunes, gives reasons to re-certify truth and abolishes error and heresy. Through reconsideration and reassessment, traditional values and familiar ideas will be proven worthy of protection or worthy of rejection.

Indeed, until re-thinking is done, all tenets, doctrines and beliefs may be suspect! The much esteemed Apostle, Paul, admonishes all to **"Prove all things; hold fast that which is good." (1 Thess 5:21)** It was for this reason that the Captain of our Souls instructed me about ten years ago to seek a revelation about everything I know and accept as *the foundation for my core beliefs!* This part of my journey as a student of the Word, a man of God and as a minister and pastor was as wonderful and exciting as it was painful and frightening. It was wonderful and exciting because it took me to places that were new, life changing and spiritually challenging and revelatory. It was painful and frightening because many of the tenets and beliefs that I had been taught by people that I have revered and honored down through the years (and still hold in high esteem for their faithfulness and holiness) were beliefs I had to alter or abolish. The inexorable he attachments that we have to mentors and friends are the same attachments we place on the teachings we receive from them.

Information is just a collection of dead and unproductive facts until the life and the mission of the Revelation is placed in the mix! Information can be used *but a Revelation uses you, challenges you and changes you!*

The Revelation has this kind of influence because it is actually a *"Knowing*!" The power of a *"knowing"* is that it produces thoughts that produce actions that produce habits that become, determine and define our character in God!

The statement that Jesus made, **"Ye shall know truth and the truth shall make you free"** (John 8:32) has its basis in the fact that when truth is revealed (not just information about the truth) that revealed truth becomes a *Knowing!* And The Knowing has such a power and life in and of itself that it demands change; it requires that the "old" give way to the "new!" The Knowing presents possibilities and innovations that cast old and time honored lifelong traditions into the seas of antiquity and obsolescence.

And because The Knowing is welcomed in the heart of the "knower" The Knowing refuses to be denied! And when The Knowing is not resisted or refused it will take the "knower" to heights heretofore unimagined!

One of the greatest taboos that the slave could breach was to learn to read! Why was it believed that a slave who could read would not be a good slave? What was the great fear that slave owners had of slaves reading a book? They knew that if the slave learned to read—the slave could come to KNOW! The slave would be overtaken by a *"KNOWING!"* The slave would be given a "REVELATION! The slave would be affected by THE TRUTH! "He, the slave master" is not better than I am! I am as deserving as he is! I KNOW THAT AM A MAN JUST LIKE HE IS! I WILL SERVE HIM NO MORE!

A Feather from the Eagle's Wing

Never let your soul suffer for something your flesh wants!

CHAPTER 6

---◆---

GOD AND HIS GODS **KNOW!**

A Key "Word Equation" for This Chapter

"<u>God doth know</u> . . . and ye shall be as gods
<u>knowing</u>!" (Gen. 3:5)

Knowing! *Knowing*! Nothing of the things that are
harbored in the mind if man is more significant than his
knowing! Satan is aware with copious clarity the power
and the benefits of *knowing*! He knows the reasons that he
inspired the slave master in early America to deny his slaves
the freedom to learn to read! For, reading would plant seeds
of *knowing* in the heart of the slave that are not conducive
to one being content to live in subjection to another. *Once a
revelation has taken root in one's heart, that **Knowing** (by its
nature) prevents one* from remaining unchanged! ***Knowing***
attracts change, newness and difference to the knower just
as the odor of your favorite food attracts you to it and the
benefits and consequences of eating it!

When we realize that a revelation (true *knowing*) truly changes us and when we know the value of Divine changes in our lives, the questions beg to be asked, "How far are we to take this *knowing?* And is there an end to the possibilities of what we can become?

First, I must remind you, Precious Hearts, *of a most profound truth!* **All that the serpent said to First Mother, Eve, in the Garden of Eden was not a lie!** Remember, a lie is not merely an untrue statement but a lie is <u>a statement that is told with intent to deceive!</u> Consider for a moment this scenario. You and another person are in a room together! No one else is in the house! When you leave the room—you leave a one hundred dollar bill on the table where you were sitting. While you are gone the other person steals the money and puts it in his pocket. When you come back into the room you ask the individual where your money is. He replies, "I don't know!" You know that no one is in the house but the two of you so you accuse him of stealing the one hundred dollars. In his defense and to make you doubt that you really did leave the money there, he exclaims, sarcastically, "Okay, yeah, Brother, I stole your money! I know that nobody is here but the two of us and I am really stupid enough to take your money *knowing* that there is no one else to blame—*but me!* Come on, Brother! Be for real!

Now, this crook actually said no less than three times the reasons you have for believing he robbed you. But He still lied! When the thief said, "Okay," yeah Brother, I stole your money!" The words were truth but his lying spirit and motive were deceptive. He agreed with you that "…nobody is here but the two of us …." And He understands as well as you do that there is no one else to blame *"but me!"* But he has not truly confessed his guilt *for the truth he told was in the very spirit of his lie!*

Oh, that old serpent in Eden did lie to Mother Eve! But some of the lies were not so much *in the words that he said* but **in the spirit of what he said! And the serpent said unto the woman, Ye shall not surely die: (Gen 3:4) For God doth know that in the day ye eat thereof, then your eyes shall be opened, and ye shall be as gods,** *knowing* **good and evil. Gen 3:5** Pay close attention to the phrases:

1. **God <u>doth know</u>**
2. **and ye shall be as gods *<u>knowing</u>*!"**

Think about it, Saints! **"<u>God doth know</u> . . . and ye shall be as gods *<u>knowing</u> . . .*!"** Those statements were not only true—they held before Eve a possibility that even in her wildest dreams she could not have entertained! She could actually, as God does, **KNOW!** Now, Eve did not know *<u>what</u> she would <u>come to know</u>* that *<u>she could not know</u>* without eating of the tree of knowledge of good and evil but she KNEW that whatever she would know **SHE WOULD *KNOW* AS GOD *KNOWS*!**

Now the Bible does not tell us exactly how Eve defined "dying" but we do know that before Adam sinned—nothing ever died! But whatever the threat that dying was to her, how comforting must it have been for her to *know* that she ". . . **shall not surely die** . . ." and what is even more, the serpent promised her ". . . **in the day ye eat thereof,**

then your eyes shall be opened, and ye shall be as gods, _knowing_ **good and evil."**

Eve knew that her natural eyes were open because she knew that she could see. But she could not even imagine what she would see if they were _"OPEN<u>ED</u>!"_ **What wonders would be hers' to behold when her eyes WERE OPENED!** All Eve knew was that when her eyes were opened—she would see **AS GOD SEES** and that was good enough for her!

Also, Eve did not know **"good and evil."** But she knew that God _KNOWS!_ However, before the serpent came and deceived her—Eve never imagined that she could _KNOW_ <u>anything</u>—LIKE GOD including what "good and evil" are<u>!</u> It was nothing less than a stroke of diabolical genius that Satan chose this temptation! He knew how much Eve loved God and wanted to please Him. It has been said that emulation is the highest form of flattery. And Satan knew that, given the opportunity, Eve would choose to be just like God! Satan knew that the temptation would be too great for First Mother to resist! As she pondered this new prospect, the revelation; The Knowing, took over her mind! For, a revelation is, after all, _a living thing!_ The new understanding over powered all of her resistance! A more wonderful possibility than she had ever imagined became achievable! The highest aspiration man could ever have hoped to accomplish washed over her and flooded her mind with potentials too grand; too magnificent and too glorious for her to at that time identify! All she knew was that she and her husband could be—LIKE GOD! Indeed, they could actually be—_"as gods"_—_KNOWING!_

30

A Feather from the Eagle's Wing

If people <u>think</u> you are ignorant—why open your mouth and remove all doubt?

CHAPTER 7

——◆●◆——

IN GOD BUT NOT IN CHRIST

A Key Understanding of this Chapter

*". . . as the heart of the giver is before God—**so is the
gift of the giver!***

I know that I am saved! I know I have been born again!
So why am I still bothered with sin and the appetites of
the flesh? Why do I find the life of Holiness to be so
burdensome? I thought that when God saved me these
problems would be over! What happened? Why can't I
believe God! Why is it so hard to get a miracle? Why can't
I forgive easily? And why do I still have anger problems!
Why am I still so afraid! Why am I still so judgmental and
so afraid of being judged? Even though I wouldn't admit
it to anyone then, before God saved me, I felt that I was
not "as good as" other people and now that I am saved—I
still feel that I am not "as good as" most of the Saints! Why
can't I love my enemies like Jesus did? Why don't I pay my
debts like I know I should? Why is it so hard to forgive?
What do people see in me that make them bring ideas and

opportunities to me that I am trying to forsake? And why can't I forsake those divinely forbidden things? Ever dealt with any of these issues? Well, my friend, read on!

Focal Verse for this Chapter's Subject

Rom 8:9 **But ye are not in the flesh, but in the Spirit, if so be that the Spirit of God dwell in you. Now <u>if any man have not the Spirit of Christ, he is none of his.</u>**

Rom 8:5 **For they that are after the flesh do mind the things of the flesh; but they that are after the Spirit the things of the Spirit.**

Rom 8:6 **For to be carnally minded *is* death; but to be spiritually minded *is* life and peace.**

Rom 8:7 **Because the carnal mind *is* enmity against God: for it is not subject to the law of God, neither indeed can be.**

Rom 8:8 **So then they that are in the flesh cannot please God.**

Rom 8:9 **But ye are not in the flesh, but in the Spirit, if so be that the Spirit of God dwell in you. Now if any man have not the Spirit of Christ, he is none of his.**

****

Rom 8:5 For they that are <u>after the flesh </u>do mind the things of the flesh; but they that are after the Spirit the things of the Spirit.

"...<u>After </u>the flesh"

The word, "after" is from a Greek word, "kata" which means (among other things) *"about, naturally of"* and *"according to."* Now, they who live according to what they are "about" "naturally" are living ". . . **after the flesh.**" These people do **"<u>mind</u> the things of the flesh."** To these people the first remedy in a crisis is earthly, carnal and logical. They are in tune with things earthly more than things Heavenly! Indeed, they may even check Heavenly things out against the earthly standards to see where and how the Heavenly can fit into their earthly agendas. When the earthly and the Heavenly clash in the lives of those who are ". . . **after the flesh,**" more often than not, it is the Heavenly that will have to make the compromise. It is the Heavenly that will be changed. If they make a shift in their judgments or standards for living—the shift will be away from the Heavenly and toward the earthly. Those benefits that result in earthly honor and prestige will be valued more highly than Spiritual rewards and gains. Those things that affect the senses and human emotions are given the highest priorities, and even earthly times and schedules take the forefront in terms of when one minds the things of the flesh.

It must be ever remembered that *"<u>the mind is the thermostat</u> and <u>the body is the thermometer</u> of the emotions of man!"* Regarding those structures that men live, work and play in thermostat sets and controls the room temperature and the thermometer records the room temperature. Mentally, the mind sends signals to the body to act according to the severity and the type of a stimulus (the room temperature) and gives orders that the body responds to thereby "conditioning" the emotional atmosphere. **"For as he thinketh in his heart, so *is* he."** (Pro 23:7)

Those persons who are **"after the flesh"** are **"fear and anger _magnets_"** and **"confusion and despair _magnets._"** They both attract and receive Satan's negative influences! Unbelief, suspicion and skepticism are as natural to their character as thorns on a rose bush and stink in a skunk! They who follow after flesh are always sought after by fleshly things! Every spirit that has satanic sympathies will find something in the character and the appetites of these people to latch on to. These spiritually weak-minded souls expect with the greatest and most miserable anticipation—all of the things that they loath, abhor and detest. They believe to receive **all of the ugly, mean and undesirable ends that the flesh can imagine!**

Our Lord has gone to great lengths that the Church should know the difference between the mind of the flesh and the spiritual mind. It naturally follows that He would make the Church to know the consequences for living according to a carnal mind and the rewards for living in a spiritual mind. He very graphically shows the cancerous malignity and the immeasurable sorrow of carnal-mindedness in contrast to the exquisite and superb excellence and serenity that is the hallmark of the spiritually minded!

"Unequivocal" and "explicit" are expressions that come to mind to describe the words that God uses to illustrate and describe the results of both of those lifestyles. Our appetites and our tastes, our choices and our approvals will have eternal ramifications! The reason for our preoccupation with these very personal identifiers is that they stem from and demonstrate the state of our heart. These elements decide the kinds of news and truths that give us joy and comfort! These mental governors illustrate what we relish and appreciate, tolerate and hate the most! These are regulators that speak the truth about who we are and whose side we are on, whether the Lords side or Satan's side!

So, to ascertain whether you *"mind the things of the flesh"* **or** *"the spirit"* **just ask yourself these questions:**

- ❖ Which direction do your thoughts move with the greatest anticipation—to the fleshly and earthly things or to the things of God?
- ❖ What does your mind linger on with the greatest longings and yearnings—things temporal or things eternal?
- ❖ The things that God brings into your life as opportunities *to grow* and *to become*—<u>**do you see them as tests and challenges?**</u>

- ❖ Are you most known for earthly sophistication or spiritual wisdom in terms of:

  - ○ the latest secular songs, books, movies, sports stats, TV programming and earthly gossip, o God's Plan of Salvation, scriptures announcing Heaven's hopes for the world, heroes of the Faith, the believer's victories and Satanic losses.

❖ Are you more familiar with earth's celebrities or Heaven's heroes?
❖ Do you spend more time on the phone, texting or emailing unsaved friends or saved Brothers and Sisters in Christ?

". . . But to be carnally minded *is* death; (Rom 8:6)

Please notice that there is no mention of the process of dying! Dying is not the issue because the Apostle is not simply speaking of a lack of life! He is addressing DEATH and all of its properties and abilities to siphon the life from and destroy the life in others! Those who are carnally minded are themselves DEAD and they have the influence on others that leaves them dead as well! In other words, the carnal are not merely dead—they are DEATH DEALING SOULS!

It should never be estimated that carnal living is equal to or better than spiritual dying! Those who allow themselves to be carnally minded will often think themselves to be more alive than everyone else. They will, at times, become laws to themselves and feel superior to all who are not likeminded.

To be carnally minded is to have approved and sanctioned sin and every thought that is counter to holy things! There is NO approving of sin without disapproving Righteousness! The carnal mind says to Right, "Be thou wrong!" It says to wrong, "Be thou right!" Thus, even when God has administered all of the Love that he can mete out with His judgment (and remain Righteous) the sentence is still DEATH! Actually, when life has been rejected there is only one alternate choice and it is—DEATH! Note 1st Tim. 5:6, **"But she that liveth in pleasure is dead while she liveth."** No soul is more dead than the carnal soul which is DEAD WHILE "... IT ... LIVETH IN PLEASURE!"

"... But to be spiritually minded ..." (Rom. 8:6 (b))

Now, let us visit the other side of the coin. "... **to be spiritually minded** ..." is to have the mind that Adam and Eve had before they were evicted from Eden. To love and appreciate; approve and adore both the Creator and His Ways is what it means to be spiritually minded. God never intended for the soul of man to be separated from the Spirit of God (though in His Omniscience He knew that it would be). God "... **breathed into his nostrils the breath of life; and man became a living soul."** (Gen. 2:7)

It must be mentioned that when God, "...**breathed into his nostrils the breath of life,"** God breathed into man's nostrils—GOD! Just as when you breathe into someone's nostrils after you have bitten into an onion—you will breathe into his nostrils the essence of the onion! Yuck! So it is that God breathed into Adam's nostrils and Adam "... **became a living soul."** When Adam sinned, there were some things that his offspring lost in body soul and spirit! Humanity lost its Holiness and Righteousness but retained the capacity to be incomplete without it. Mankind also kept a longing for that *"something"* that people are looking for *"in all the wrong places!"* They search for it in drugs, alcohol, in marriages and other relationships, in sex in power and prestige and try to search every place they haven't yet looked! Man is still seeking that oneness and that intimacy that Adam and Eve had with the Father in the Garden of Eden. Man is yet searching for that union of heart and mind; that tranquility and peace that only the raw Presence of God in one's heart can provide! We, the Children of God, must get the word out to the world that the life and the peace that is eluding them can only be found in one becoming **"spiritually minded!"**

Rom 8:7 Because the carnal mind *is* enmity against God: for it is not subject to the law of God, neither indeed can be.

O Consenting to remain *of the old man* <u>makes one an enemy of God!</u>

> O **Because the carnal mind *is* enmity against God:**
>
> > ■ Only from the heart of God can the *Knowing* come of the full import of this truth: ". . . <u>the carnal mind is enmity against God!</u>"
> >
> > ■ To be born in sin is not of man's purposeful doing—but the choice to be carnal places the responsibility at man's doorstep!

- It is bad enough to be *"dead in your sins"* (Eph. 2:1) because of being born into that lowly estate) but it is even worse to be of a carnal mind because you have chosen against being of a spiritual mind.

- The carnal mind is not just a "dead" man—he is a "devilish" man!

o "... for it is not subject to the law of God, neither indeed can be. Rom 8:7

  o To *be "dead in your sins"* is bad and to have a carnal mind is worse—but to have a mind that **"is not subject to the law of God, neither indeed can be"** *is infinitely worse!*

    - The carnal mind is diametrically opposed to everything Holy!

    - That soul that is not subject to the law of God and never can be is **not** merely at odds with or in simple disagreement with God but opposes Him openly and blatantly! That individual is not just an enemy of God but is the personification of enmity itself!

    - Tragically, this is not a person who has decided that God may be necessary in some people's lives but "I don't feel a need for Him." This person actually is at war with God at the highest and most significant levels!

- This evil has placed itself above the Mind, the Will, the Authority and the Power of The Almighty God!

- There is no more insolent and disrespectable, brazenly contemptible and impertinent disregard and slander for God than this mindset demonstrates!

- Consider that even mortal enemies can become friends but enmity can find no basis for friendship at any level!

- Most assuredly, the Child of the King must fight the sickness and the wicked weakness of carnal mindedness with every strength and power he can marshal to this defense!

Rom 8:8 So then they that are in the flesh cannot please God.

Those who are yielded to the will of Satan cannot please God in that state because, first of all, wickedness is an affront to God! Sin is always planned and inspired by the devil! The "old man" (the flesh) is always at the beck-and-call of its lord. Hence, the powerful truthfulness of Jesus when He declared to the Jews, **"Ye are of your father the devil, and the lusts of your father ye will do."** (John 8:44KJV)

If the flesh, in its imperfection, accidently did something that falls into the category of "things God desires"—God is still not pleased because *without faith it is impossible to please God!* **The sacrifice of the wicked** *is* **an abomination to the LORD (Pro 15:8)** so that wicked one who inadvertently and accidently did something right will ultimately be rejected because *as the heart of the giver is before God—***so is the gift of the giver!**

A Feather from the Eagle's Wing

"Any man who is wrapped up in himself makes a pretty small package."

My father, the late Elder Samuel D. Tolbert Sr. told this to me.

CHAPTER 8

———◆►●◄◆———

ARE YOU <u>IN</u> THE SPIRIT OR <u>OF</u> THE FLESH?

A Key Question of This Chapter

Who knows you as "servant" God or Satan, the Great Deceiver?

If I am saved, who then, claims me? WHO AM I and WHOSE AM I? The esteemed, Apostle, Paul asserts in Roman 8:9, **"But ye are not in the flesh, but in the Spirit, if so be that the Spirit of God dwell in you. Now <u>if any man have not the Spirit of Christ, he is none of his.</u>"**

We all know that we are spirit beings dwelling in a house of flesh! But there is a vast difference between living *<u>in</u>* **the Spirit** and living *<u>in</u>* **the flesh!** The deciding factor as to *where one dwells* is determined by *who <u>dwells in you</u> <u>and in whom you dwell!</u>* The word, "dwelling" as used in this work is more than merely taking up residence. It is to take ownership of, take responsibility for, to dominate and to rule. If you are dwelling in the flesh and if Satan is living in you with all of his devilish ideas, cravings, violence and mischief—**you are living in the flesh!** If it is God living in you and inspiring you to all of the fruit of the Spirit—**you are living in the Spirit!**

Accept the truths of the following verses:

Rom 6:16 Know ye not, that to whom ye yield yourselves servants to obey, his servants ye are to whom ye obey; whether of sin unto death, or of obedience unto righteousness?

Rom 6:17 But God be thanked, that ye were the servants of sin, but ye have obeyed from the heart that form of doctrine which was delivered you.

Rom 6:18 Being then made free from sin, ye became the servants of righteousness.

****

Know ye not, that to whom ye yield yourselves servants to obey, his servants ye are to whom ye obey; whether of sin unto death, or of obedience unto righteousness? (Rom 6:16)

The basic foundation for action in an American court of law is the truth that is supported by evidence! In the matter before our hearts this day the standard of acceptability is no less! Let us examine the evidence to prove whether you are living in the Spirit or in the flesh! Who has ownership of your members? To whom have you yielded yourselves! Who knows you as "servant?" Is it God or the Great

Deceiver? To whom do you bow in obeisance and bend yourself in servitude and obedience? Is it the Almighty God or that defeated foe, Satan?

When people yield themselves they usually give way to that which is greater in some way. Sometime the greater is defined as deserving of superior greater honor. Sometimes greater is defined as stronger and more dangerous. Oft times it is all about social position and authority. So the scripture has its basis in the fact that whomsoever you yield yourselves to—you are bowing to in humility and servitude. You have consented to be their servant!

This truth prevails whether one yields to that cruel task master, Satan or to the Great Lover of our souls, Jesus Christ! But know thou, that whatever you decide—there will be Heaven to enjoy forever or there will be Hell to pay forever. The choice is yours!

Yield to this scrutiny of self one bit further, please. Have you surrendered to "...**sin unto death**..."or are you acting in "...**obedience**..." to God "...**unto righteousness?**"

But God be thanked, that ye were the servants of sin, but ye have obeyed from the heart that form of doctrine which was delivered you. (Rom. 6:17)

After such a weighty discussion as was just finished, it is so refreshing to enter into another dialogue and one that begins with, **"But God be thanked...!"** The emotions of the valiant and courageous Apostle, Paul, have for a long time captured my attention! Whether the mood and the passion be of gratitude, joy, sorrow or confusion—I know that he was not one to whimper and cry in weakness or to rejoice and give thanks from a heart of gladness—<u>haphazardly</u>. So, when this thankfulness virtually gushes out of him as if pent up in him for far too long, I take great notice of it! These words, **"But God be thanked . . ."** exploded out of him (as an expletive from the heart of a passionate and greatly agitated mind) and quickly prepared me to expect a most wonderful an exquisite thought! And my anticipation was not the least bit disappointed!

". . . that <u>ye were</u> the servants of sin . . . ,"

The acknowledgement here is that our servitude to sin is in our past. Here, we are given to recognize that our transgressions no longer can hold sway over our mind! We are herein allowed to rejoice that our past with its sins and shame are completely and absolutely ineffectual in our present day and can have no more influence on our tomorrows than a shadow's touch! This is a beautiful carol to be sung to comfort us and send us to a restful peaceful sleep. This truth is a sound that we will hear in our dark days of confusion, loss and despair. And it speaks to us as one whose voice will always show us the way back home! This heartfelt realization is also a song of victory to send us off confidently into battle and is the refrain that we will use on the battlefield—as a battle cry!

". . . <u>ye were </u>the servants of sin . . . !" It is now that we can know that we are vindicated! We are justified! It is truly, at long last, a fact of life that—*We are without blame!* Our sinful past is better than erased! It is completely and eternally covered by and obliterated by the Blood of Jesus Christ which means *not only that are we forgiven by the*

Love of God **but that the final debt for our sins is paid!** Now, none, whether man, angel or demon can hold those sins to our charge! For, all of Heaven recognizes and celebrates our freedom! And what is the greatest of all joys is that our Savior; our Redeemer and our Souls Greatest Lover rejoices with us in our liberty!

"... but ye have obeyed from the heart ..."

As all service for the Lord must be "heart service" so must all obedience to the Lord be from the heart. Only service from the heart can produce worship **"in spirit and in truth!"** (See John 4:24) Obeying from the heart insures that service will be done to the maximum of the server's love, devotion and spiritual creativity and will be seasoned and tempered by the Grace of God!

"... that form of doctrine which was delivered you."

To obey from the heart is to act from a virtual sea of potential. For, the depths of the heart can only be measured by the responding performance of the body and soul. And when the soul has understood, received, appreciated and surrendered to "... **that form of doctrine which was delivered you,"** the obedient heart will *KNOW* the wonder of God, the perfection of God and will love the law, the Grace and the Spirit of God!

Being then made free from sin, (Rom 6:18)

All who are free from sin are actually **freed** from sin! We were saved from the original sin to which we were all born and the sins that we had committed! Though we still need to be *made free* from the sins that live in potential while resting in our "old man," that is *the flesh!* This freeing is done in a three step process **after salvation has come**. The three are:

- ⬦ Put off the "old man" Deny the flesh preeminence and control!
- ⬦ Be renewed in the Spirit of you mind!
- ⬦ Put on the "new man" and live by the "renewed" mind! *(This is discussed at great length later in the book.)*

"... ye became the servants of righteousness."

Jesus **"learned ... obedience by the things which he suffered ...,"** Heb 5:8, (not that He was ever disobedient) but He developed and was improved and became so longsuffering that He was able to surrender to the death at Calvary which was His most difficult trial. He did this in order to fulfill all Righteousness so we could become the servants of righteousness.

Now, **"... if any man have not the Spirit of Christ, <u>he is none of his.</u>"** It is in this passage of scripture that there is made clear a difference between having **"... the Spirit of God ..."** and having **"... the spirit of Christ."** There are those who do have the Spirit of God but *because they don't yield themselves to the influences of the Spirit of God and seek to know God and be developed after His Likeness*—**they don't appreciate or emphasize the nature and the character of Christ.** Many well meaning Christians make the Righteousness of God more important than the Love, Mercy and Grace of God. These often are all about restrictions and taboos and seem to completely lose sight of the liberties and freedoms that are given by God to the Children of God to for their enjoyment and His praise.

Having the Spirit of God (the Holy Ghost) enables the born again believer to walk according to the standards of holiness and exemplify righteousness in contrast to the standards that were observed and lived when we walked according the **weak and beggarly elements** (Gal 4:9) of the sinful world. Additionally, it is the Spirit of God that is the Power by which miracles are wrought by the faith of the True Believer. (See acts 1:8)

The "Spirit of Christ," *the Love Spirit*, is the part of Jesus' nature that caused Him to love and show compassion; to give and forgive; believe for those who had no faith and see beyond the veil of Earth's realities to Heaven's potentials. The Spirit of God used the Blood of Jesus to **"blot out the handwriting of ordinances that was against us, which was contrary to us, and took it out of the way, nailing it to his cross."** (Col 2:14 KJV) Indeed, it is the Spirit of Christ that causes the Love of God to see His people through the shed Blood of Jesus Christ and count them worthy of all of the benefits of His Presence while they are on this Earth. And the Love Spirit makes available to the Faithful all of the joys and treasures of Heaven.

It was the Love Spirit that did not allow Jesus to pass by a funeral procession and ignore the grieving cries of the widow of Nain. It was also the Spirit of Christ that did not allow Jesus to rebuke the "Woman With the Issue of Blood" when she violated Jewish law and touched Him to receive her healing. The Love Spirit caused Jesus to love

Lazarus enough to come too late to heal Him but just in time to raise him from the dead!

The learned Apostle, Paul, admonishes the church to **"Walk in the Spirit . . . ."** (Gal 5:16 KJV) It must be accepted by all who desire to walk with God that there is a reality that is called, "In the Spirit."

To be "in the spirit" means that the Spirit of God is not a visitor in you. Nor is the Spirit in you as an interloper or an intruder but the Spirit is a welcomed resident in your heart, taking the charge of your heart as one who lives there and has authority over what goes on there!

". . . He that dwelleth in love dwelleth in God, and God in him. (1st John 4:16) The key word that must be mentioned in this verse is *"dwelleth."* The Love of God for His Children must be reciprocal! The Love of God longs to be one with the loving heart of the loving Children of God! They that dwell in God and they who reside and take ownership of God do it only as they are afforded the privilege by the Love of God! Love is an indwelling force with an outward manifestation. Love is also a place from which the heart calls, reaches and changes the world that is on the outside of love! Since God is Love—all those who live in God live in Love and all who live in Love live in God!

Now, **". . . if any man have not the Spirit of Christ, he is none of his,"** (Rom. 8:9) thus, the Father only identifies Himself with those who have the Spirit of Christ! So, it is possible to have the Spirit of God and not have the Spirit of Christ! Don't forget, Student of the Word, the Apostle,

John, said, **"My little children, these things write I unto you** .... (1Jn 2:1) By this term of endearment and John's ownership of his responsibility for them, *"My little children.* You see, he is talking to the Church and it is possible to have the Spirit of God and be devoid of the Spirit of Christ! This is the reason that the Child of God must **"... put off the old man ... ,"** be **"... renewed in the spirit of your mind ..."** and **"... put on the new man which, after God, is created in righteousness and true holiness!"** While the believer may have had sins washed away and even been Spirit filled and has the spiritual DNA to prove that the spiritual birth did occur, WITHOUT THE SPIRIT OF CHRIST IN HIM—God say's, **"he is none of His!**

However, do not be dismayed! God had a reason for inspiring Paul to write that we can be renewed in the spirit of our mind! We can put on the new man!

A Feather from the Eagle's Wings

"Don't be so full of yesterday that there is no room for today."

CHAPTER 9

———⟫•⟨———

TAKE IT ALL OFF—PUT IT ALL ON!

A Key to a Little Known Truth
Concerning Spiritual Development

There is a three step process of development that must be done <u>after a sinner is "regenerated."</u>

Eph 4:22 That ye put off concerning the former conversation the old man, which is corrupt according to the deceitful lusts;

Eph 4:23 And be renewed in the spirit of your mind;

Eph 4:24 And that ye put on the new man, which after God is created in righteousness and true holiness.

Am I truly saved? What happened to the **"new creature"** that I am supposed to be **now that I am ". . . in Christ?"** And if ". . . **old things <u>are</u> passed away and all things <u>are</u> become new . . . ,"** according to 2nd Cor. 5:17, *where, then, is the newness? **And why is so much "old" still in my life?***

Also, if the "newness" is not evident then **am I "new" after all?** Again I ask, *"Am I truly saved?"* What happened to me?!

The "happening" actually occurred thousands of years before we were born. Adam was created a perfect man but he traded his perfection for the pleasure of eating from the tree of Knowledge of Good and Evil. So, when we were born, **we inherited <u>all that he became after his fall</u>!** There is sin that we commit today that Adam never committed so we did not inherit each individual sin from Adam! But what we did get from him was the potential, proclivity, weakness, lust and appetite to commit sin!

Spiritually, there is a need for every Christian to "upgrade" your spirit man. When you were first born again, you were truly a "new creature!" Old things *had all passed away* and all things *did become new*. You see, in every case of a born again experience, we all had to completely surrender our lives, identities, aspirations, attitudes and everything that makes us who and what we are.

Old things passed away and all things became new. But I believe that we can all agree that things did not stay that way! Somehow, *the Old Man was revived!* Perhaps as old situations cropped up again in your life you reverted back to old habits and ways of evaluating and dealing with them **according to your former behavior.** Or maybe someone reminded you of an experience, an injustice, a dream or pleasure that was a part of the Old Man and the old life but *as sure as the sun is in the sky—the Old Man was revived!* You did not realize it but *the Old Man had never really left you—*you left it! *You got saved **but the Old***

Man didn't! The next thing you knew was—you were again dealing with most of the former attitudinal weaknesses, fleshly desires, worldly entertainments, negative feelings and the like that you dealt with before you were saved.

Now, you may find that you have to struggle to swallow some of the same things that you easily embraced that pleased God when you were in your spiritual infancy. And you now may begin to wonder if it really *"takes all of that"* to get to Heaven. After you were first born again you didn't try to see how much you *had to do for God*—**you did all that He did not stop you from doing!** Now, your life seems to be marked with evidences that you are fast becoming "double minded" and carnally minded! Don't get me wrong, though, I know that you still want to go to Heaven! But there are times now when you may wonder at the high cost of Heaven! Though, *before the Old Man raised his head,* you were only aware of **the high cost of Hell!** Now, you may slowly began to remember *or you may be reminded* of all the many things of the world that you had forever forsaken *(or so you thought)*. You may remember things that were said to you and things said about you that had a negative effect on you; all of the things that you know you were never able to accept with grace from people. You may remember all of your "pet peeves" and all of your quirks, idiosyncrasies and you now find that once again people are "pushing your buttons! You can come to the place where you begin to rehearse in your *Old Man's mind* things that you always felt were unfair and unjust that others did to you! Maybe you will begin to add up the score card and realize that you have invested more in others than they have ever invested in you and you now want reparations and payback. Since you know that **they** (*whoever they are*) will never pay you back—you satisfy yourself with telling your tale of woe to any who will listen to you.

Then, there are things **you did for the love of God**—but now, *because of Old Man logic*, you feel that ***you were taken advantage of!***

THE OLD MAN IS PERFECTLY WILLING TO LIVE IN GOD'S PERMISSIVE WILL! THE NEW MAN ONLY DESIRES TO LIVE IN GOD'S PERFECT WILL—PERFECTLY!

Yes, you are reminded of things that you enjoyed in the world; things that you loved to do and things you intended to do but never got around to it and you have begun to try to find a way to make them fit into your "holy" life!

Is it worth it? Look at the terrible price you are now paying! You lost the real *joy of your salvation* and you sacrificed your *peace that passeth understanding*. But despite *how worldly you have become* **you have learned how to be "spiritual" around other church folk.** You traded genuineness and authenticity for pretence and façade! You traded your intimate relationship with God for an acquaintance with Him! Some of you still talk to God on a regular basis because that is your habit. That is also something that you are prone to tell others about because (in your mind) it affirms and proves that you are still a Child of God. Others of you don't talk to God very much anymore (except to tell him your needs) because you are ashamed of your heart and your life before him.

But you are not the only one who is affected by your negative change. The world no longer looks at you with hope and longing. They used to watch the way they talked around you and apologize for any inappropriate words they said in your presence **but they don't anymore.** And every once in a while you catch them looking at you *when they thought you were not looking* and you wonder at the sadness and confusion in their eyes and the frown on their face.

Do you understand that they thought you were their billboard that advertised their way out of the hell and the madness that is their life? ***Do you finally get it?*** When they suggested things that they knew you shouldn't participate in ***it was only to reassure themselves that there was hope for them after all!*** Did you know how much they wanted you to say, "No?" And how much they wish you had? But *you were too busy **catching up** * on all the things **they were trying to give up!** You were **too busy trying to make up for lost time** when they <u>were trying to redeem the time they had already lost!</u>

All of this was because **you learned that "God is Love"** and because you were living in the Old Man and by its operating system (the flesh) **<u>you took the Love of God too far!</u>** You abused the Grace of God and worshipped and praised God all the while you ignored the sin in your life!

Do you get it yet? Do you know what you need? Are you ready to finally become who you were meant to be all the time? Are you ready for your "makeover?" ***<u>Are you ready for your "Upgrade?"</u>***

The Upgrade

Being saved is not enough—you must "put on the New Man." This is what it means to be in Christ. Brothers and Sisters in Christ, you will never live up to your full potential in God until you "put off the Old Man and are renewed in the spirit of your mind and then put on the New Man!

Because of Adam's sin in Eden, all we must now deal with the *"old man"* (the Adamic nature)! *There is a three step process of development that must be done **after a sinner is "regenerated."*** The three steps are:

1. "Put off the "old man" (the fleshly or Adamic nature)
2. Renew the spirit of your mind.
3. Put on the "New man!"

You, who are computer literate, know that there is often a need to upgrade your computer. As your need for a computer changes you may need to change your technology! You may need more memory, or hard drive storage or even a new video card and sound card. Your computer may run too slow for the amount of information you are transferring. You may need to upgrade your fan motor because the unit may be running too hot! There are all sorts of reasons for upgrading the computer.

You may also be aware that every computer must have an "OS" (operating System.) The operating system is the brain of the computer containing the language that the computer will talk and understand in and the OS (Operating System) gives orders that the Computer will obey and at the same time it executes the commands that the user gives it. If you put software program that is written in a language or a format that the computer is not configured for in the disk drive the computer will not be able to read the software or execute the commands on the disk. If that happens either the disk will not work at all or the results will be unpredictable.

Similarly, both the "Old Man" and the New Man need an "operating system" in order to make the spiritual body function! Now, the OS of the Old Man is the flesh and its lustful appetites with Satan as the programmer. The Holy Spirit is the OS for the New Man. It is no wonder that Jesus told the Pharisees and other Jews, **"Ye are of *your* father the devil, and the lusts of your father <u>ye will do</u>. He was a murderer from the beginning, and abode not in the truth, because <u>there is no truth in him.</u> When he speaketh a lie, he speaketh of his own: for <u>he is a liar,</u> and <u>the father of it.</u>** (Joh 8:44)

Jesus has provided the OS for the New Man. He says, **"For as many as are <u>led by the Spirit of God</u>, they are the sons of God.** (Rom 8:14) So, they are sons of God who are led by His spirit. The New Man can no more follow the dictates of the flesh than the flesh can be led by the Spirit of God! They are from entirely different worlds, cultures and languages! The Old Man must be driven while the New Man must be led! The Old Man must see "instant gratification" and the New Man will opt for "delayed gratification!" The Old Man has little patience while the New Man is longsuffering and patient! The Old Man loves to play more than pray and the New Man loves to pray more than play! And the Old Man is the residue (flesh) of the former life that is left in every Christian and that residue is what the devilish things of the world are attracted to! And it is the thing in the Christian that attracts devilish things! The Old Man is the only part of the Christian entity that Satan, his demons and the world can get a grip on! The Old Man must be "put off" and the New Man must be "put on!"

First in the three-step process of spiritual development is to ". . . **put off concerning the former conversation the old man, which is corrupt according to the deceitful lusts. (**Eph 4:22) The flesh, called, "the old man," must be ". . . **put off** . . . !" This putting off is not done just by ridding oneself of fleshly *things* but by denouncing the world and its sinful and abominable worldliness. Yes, we must ". . . **put off the old man** . . . . (Col. 3:10) and actually surrender to the *"Knowing!"*

This process must be done purposefully, and systematically! Make a list of all of the core values, thinking and doings that were really of the Old Man! Then refer to that list every time a "crisis" occurs and these negative behaviors show up! When they show up—**you cut them down!** As you cut them down you seek God for a mindset that God approves and search the scriptures for the attitude, game plan and strength to deal with them as our Christ would!

The **"old man"** *is,* to say the least, **corrupt"**. And it is **corrupt** by reason of ". . . **the deceitful lusts.**" The lusts are deceitful because they always promise greater satisfaction and pleasure than will occur! The deceitful lusts don't tell of the misery, self loathing and guilt that will wreck the peace of those whose conscience (being activated) will eventually inflict on them! They also conceal the fact that the sinner will have Hell to pay for sins committed. The old man is not sanctified!

Eph. 4:23 And be renewed in the spirit of your mind . . . .

One might wonder, "If all men were born in sin with a fleshly 'old man,' how a mind can be <u>re</u>-*newed* that has never been new?" The Psalmist, David, when giving his explanation to Nathan, the prophet, concerning David's sin with bath-sheba when "*. . . he lay with her . . . ,*" *(See 2nd Sam. 11:3)* reasoned, **"Behold, I was <u>shapen in iniquity</u>; and <u>in sin did my mother conceive me.</u>"** (Psa. 51:5) To paraphrase David, "I came into this world spoiled! I, being **"conceived"** in sin, **am the product of sin!** The Apostle, Paul, confesses to the church that he was **"sold under sin!"** in Rom. 7:14(b). *(Discussed later in Chapter 32)*

The second step in the process of spiritual development is to ". . . **be renewed in the spirit of your mind."** (Eph 4:23) To be renewed in the spirit of our mind is a consideration that is of paramount importance! Consider this illustration. If your mind is not "renewed" you may have the strength to do what is right—but will not have the power and authority to embrace right and do it in the right spirit! You will then obey in a spirit of disobedience! Consider the following illustration.

"I'm standing up on the Inside!"

The little seven year old terror, still in his Spider man pajamas was running around the coffee table screaming the sound of a police car siren. As he completed his turn around the final corner of the table he tore up the hardwood stairs and headed for his bedroom! He ran into the bedroom and with a much practiced hand slammed the door behind him! Sliding to a stop just in front of his night stand, he grabbed the TV remote and pushed the red button to turn the television on. It came on blasting the Transformers cartoon at full volume! After watching the cartoon for about three minutes he took off again. Ripping the door open, he headed down the hall to the stairs. He pounded down the stairs yelling at the top of his voice, "C'mon Autobots! The Decepticons are comin'!"

His feet hammered the stairs as he jumped the last three stairs and ran down the hall into the kitchen. His father and mother were still sitting at the table this Saturday morning. With his usual speedy spoon he had quickly eaten his Count Chocula cereal, wolfed down the rest of his breakfast and began his high speed day. Now, his father looked over his news paper and said, Ernie, this is the last time I am going to tell you to sit down and play with your toys quietly.

"Yes sir!" He replied as he ran around the table and headed back down the hall to the living room! With a loud, "Decepticons, you're goin' down!" Ernie misjudged his distance as he started around the coffee table and the beautiful glass eagle centerpiece went crashing to the floor. The glass eagle shattered all over the hardwood floor. His parents ran into the living room with his mother in the lead. "Ernie! Are you all right?" she demanded to know. "Yes Maam!" He answered.

His mother and father looked him over closely and saw that he was indeed alright.

"Come here, young man!" she said as she took him by his arm and led him to the nearest corner of the room. She placed little Ernie on his little stool in his timeout spot facing the corner and said, "Now you stay there until you can stop running around!"

As his mother turned to walk back to the kitchen she heard Ernie defiantly whisper under his breath, *"But I'm standing up on the inside!"*

Isa 1:19   If ye be willing and obedient, ye shall eat the good of the land:

Little Ernie was obedient! He sat down in the corner! But he did so under protest and duress! It is not enough for you to be obedient—*you must be willing!* For, God does not judge actions alone—God judges the heart! To be "obedient" can stem from a fear of consequences rather than from a heartfelt desire to be righteousness! But to be "willing" comes from a heart that is surrendered to God and a love for Holiness!

Whereas the influence of the "old man" (the flesh) may provide for one being obedient, the old man will not always prove to be of a willing heart! The flesh will usually have an ulterior or a hidden motive. In contrast, one who has been renewed in the spirit of one's mind will find that love of God and Holiness will be the impetus and drive that motivates obedience.

When we get the understanding into our spirits that "the living revelation," (true *Knowing*) refuses to be frustrated or hindered—**we will anticipate being renewed; we will expect to be changed and we cannot rest until *The Knowing* has done its work!** It is the nature and the purpose of *The Knowing* to take us into divine potential by affecting a new order; a new mindset and a new outlook on life and God—*in our spirit!*

Without being **"renewed in the spirit of your mind"** you will never be able to produce the fruit of the Spirit! The carnal mind can only produce carnal works! Even when the carnal mind influences one to do what is right—the purpose will be wrong! Additionally, without being **"renewed in the spirit of your mind"** your New Man will have no "brain" or operating system to work from! The New Man cannot use the mentality, code of conduct and the lowly standards of acceptability that are the hallmark and the basic characteristics of the Old Man.

It is right to be kind and demonstrate gentleness, longsuffering, goodness and faith! But to do those things just to manipulate a person so as to take advantage of that person **is all kinds of wrong! The Old Man knows what is right** but **does not always honor what is right! It knows what is just *but will not always defend it!*** Remember Micah 6:8, **"He hath shewed thee, O man, what *is* good; and what doth the LORD require of thee, but to do justly, and to love mercy, and to walk humbly with thy God?"** This standard is not just for Israel whom God was speaking to but for the whole of mankind! Certainly the unregenerated Old Man knows **"what *is* good"** and **"what the Lord doth require** which is **to do justly, and to love**

mercy, and to walk humbly with thy God." But it is sorely lacking in the ability to consistently make the Holy choice. Hence, you have the dire need to be **"renewed in the spirit of your mind"** after which you must **"put on the new man, which after God is created in righteousness and true holiness."**

Being "saved" does not mean that you are righteous in all of your doings and does not mean that you will live Holy. What it does mean is that you were made to be righteous by reason of the Blood of Jesus that covers your sin. And you are now qualified and authorized to **become** Righteous in your lifestyle and you can develop spiritually into a Holy vessel of God wherein you can live Holy.

Again, I say, this is why *we must first* **"put off concerning the former conversation the old man, which is corrupt according to the deceitful lusts"** and secondly, **"be renewed in the spirit of your mind."** Following that you must **"put on the new man, which after God is created in righteousness and true holiness."**

The third stage in the process is to "... **Put on the new man, which after God is created in righteousness and true holiness."** Note that we are not only instructed to **"put on the new man"** but are apprised as to the character and the quality of righteousness and true holiness that is the nature of the New Man! God Himself is used as the Pattern, Template and Prototype.

My father, the late Elder Samuel D. Tolbert Sr., while teaching and preaching was known to tell stories to illustrate the points he wanted to make. While teaching a

Bible Class at our Church, told the story of "The Truth vs. The Lie." The following is my version of this story.

As the story goes, one day The Truth and The Lie went "skinny dipping." Now they didn't go together because even though The Lie will walk with anybody, the Truth will never walk with anybody who isn't all about the truth! So, each of them went to the old swimming hole that was called the Old Mill Pond. They each enjoyed the water but The Lie got tired of swimming before the Truth did. So, The Lie got out of the water and looked over at the bush that he had draped his clothes on. He saw that his clothes were ragged and dirty and smelly. He then looked over at the bush where the Truth laid his clothes. He saw that the Truth's clothes were pristine white and neatly folded and The Lie felt an almost uncontrollable urge to vomit! Those clothes of The Truth's looked so clean and honest that the Lie felt an involuntary shudder suddenly and violently shake his body in a hard spasm.

The Lie looked back at his clothes with utter delight at their condition. It had taken him a long time to get his clothes that dirty, wrinkled and stinky! His mouth virtually drooled with joy as he looked lovingly at his raggedy garments!

He glanced out of the corner of his eye at the Truth who was still having a great time swimming and paying no attention to the Lie. Then The Lie thought up a trick that would fool everybody into believing the biggest and the juiciest lie of them all! After all, he was The Lie and the father of every lie that was ever told! Quickly, he fought down the urge to puke up every bit of his breakfast as he snatched the Truth's clothes up and as quick as you can say. "Tell a lie," The Lie had put Truth's clothes on and was headed back into town.

After a while, the Truth tired of swimming and got out of the water to dress and go back to town. He knew exactly where he had left his clothes but when he looked there—they were gone! The Truth knew that he was supposed to get dressed so he looked everywhere he could but his clothes were nowhere to be found. What he did find was the stinkiest, dirtiest and most ragged garments that he had ever seen in his life.

The Truth thought for a moment and made a decision! He turned his back on the Lie's clothes and marched up the hill to the road and went on into town—NAKED but still the Truth! He was the Naked Truth!

There should be something in every born again Child of God that is not satisfied with living within the fleshly constraints of the "Old Man!" It is not just that it should be beneath the born again believer to live a shallow, base and carnal life. But the nature of sin and the abominable deeds of the flesh should be things that are detestable, abhorring and against everything that the Christian stands for! The true Christian does not put sin in degrees and hold that some sins are worse than others are! To the true Christian who has "Put it All Off and Put it All on," all sin is sin and it is beneath him/her to live in such spiritual squalor! No one who has put on the New Man would choose to live in any way that the Holy Spirit and the Righteousness of God finds detestable!

A Feather From the Eagle's Wing

You will only walk as a true son of God (a god among men) to the extent that you are yielded to and led by the Almighty God!

CHAPTER 10

CAN YOU REALLY AFFORD THE "OLD MAN?"

A Key to the Purpose of this Chapter

The costs of NOT putting on the new man are many and enormous and potentially eternal!

The fact is that many in the Church still are harboring and living in attitudes, prejudices and appetites of the flesh which are clear and vital indications that they have either not:

> ➤ "put off the old man" or
> ➤ have not been "renewed in the spirit of . . ." their ". . . mind."
> ➤ have not **"put on the new man, which after God is created in righteousness and true holiness."**

Just as the fastest way to make a new batch of yogurt is to mix in a culture of a previous batch of yogurt and thereby speed up the fermentation process, Satan wants there to be some of the **"old man"** (the flesh) left in the heart of every believer. It is this carnal residual of the old and condemned nature of man that is easily identified by Satan and it also easily identifies with and is attracted to fleshly habits and potentials. These **"works of the flesh"** (Gal. 5:19) will become weights and eventually—SINS (See Heb. 12:1) that so easily beset the Saints of God!

The costs of NOT putting on the new man are many and enormous and potentially eternal!

○ When the "Old Man" is permitted to live divine potentials are frustrated because the "Old Man" resists all efforts to develop the nature of the new man **"which after God is created in righteousness and true holiness . . ."** and

  ■ without the nature of the new man you cannot understand the things of God because **"the natural man receiveth not the things of the Spirit of God: for they are foolishness unto him: neither can he know *them*, because they are spiritually discerned."** (1Cor.2:14) Also, **"the light shineth in darkness, and the darkness comprehendeth it not.** (John 1:5)

○ Supernatural and Heavenly understanding and *The Knowing* and Revelatory Principles are denied you because you won't seek God or be available for Him to anoint and appoint you to accomplish His Agenda! Remember, **"They that are after the flesh do mind the things of the flesh."** (Rom. 8:5).

○ The work of **The Knowing** is not completed by our becoming aware of our insufficiencies. But when we *submit to the anointing that is in **The Knowing*** and *allow the power of **The Knowing** to grow in us,* developing us and grooming us from the inside out *it is then that the objective of **The Knowing** is accomplished!* It is then that **the "New Man"** has been created in us to enable us to live in righteousness and true holiness!

CHAPTER 11

POTENTIALS OF THE "OLD MAN" VS. POTENTIALS OF THE "NEW MAN"

A Key Explanation for this Chapter

God assigned one of these elements in the nature of mankind to Himself and the other He appointed to Man.

Everything that has life has the ability to leave a residual of its presence on whatever it comes into contact with! This is true from the fingerprint that man leaves at the slightest touch of his finger to the slimy trail that is left by the lowly "slug." It must be understood that the **"Old Man"** and the **"New Man"** are very much alive. Thus, they will alter, in some way, everything they encounter! Each of these mindsets has its place of origin, its potentials and its agenda.

Everything that has an origin must, of necessity, have an originator! All things are made by God so, God made the "Old Man" and God made the "New Man." These He made to be part of the mental and spiritual makeup of mankind." However, God assigned one of these elements in the nature of mankind *to Himself* and the other He appointed *to Man*. The one He kept to Himself, He called the "New Man!" The one he consigned to Man, He called, the "Old Man!"

The "New Man, ". . . **which after God, is created in righteousness and true holiness . . . ,**" (Eph. 4:24) operates using a mind that has a renewed spirit and is thus the part of God in man that is the agent of God. The "New Man" personifies the heart and the core of the divine nature of God and is the Power of God in man that enables him to qualify to ". . . **do all things through Christ who strengthens** . . ." him! (Phil. 4:13) So, God fulfills His mission statement which is to give a repented and surrendered humanity, ". . . **life, and that they might have *it* more abundantly.**" (John 10:10b)

On the other hand, the "Old Man" is the representative essence of Satan's character and Satan's direct link to the mind of man. Jesus clearly saw this truth in the Pharisees when He exposed them and all who are likeminded, thusly, **"Ye are of *your* father the devil, and the lusts of your father ye will do. (**Joh 8:44) The **"Old man"** is resident in the mind of man to influence man to do accomplish *the satanic agenda* which is ". . . **to steal, and to kill, and to destroy.**"(John 10:10a)

The Apostle, Paul, wants the Body of Christ to *Know* what the **"works"** or labors of the flesh are so He lists them in Gal.5:19-21.

> ➤ Gal 5:19 Now the works of the flesh are manifest, which are *these;* Adultery, fornication, uncleanness, lasciviousness,
> ➤ Gal 5:20 Idolatry, witchcraft, hatred, variance, emulations, wrath, strife, seditions, heresies,
> ➤ Gal 5:21 Envyings, murders, drunkenness, revellings, and such like: of the which I tell you before, as I have also told *you* in time past, that they which do such things shall not inherit the kingdom of God.

It is without fear of controversy or argument of any sort from reasonable souls that I say that the **"works of the flesh"** or the **"the works of the Old Man,"** stem from the basest and the lowest of man's character and nature. Paul teaches that there are some things that the nature of a man knows and teaches. For instance, (Co 11:14) **Doth not even nature itself teach you, that, if a man have long hair, it is a shame unto him?** Also, it should resonant in the heart of every man that the **"works of the flesh"** are beneath the dignity of God's masterpiece! They are most certainly disavowed by the Word of God!

These seventeen spirits of depravity (works of the flesh) can be categorized as follows: **idolatry and witchcraft** are crimes against the first and the second commandments. **Adultery, fornication, uncleanness and lasciviousness** fracture the seventh commandment. Still others are sins against our fellowman: *hatred, variance, emulations, wrath, strife, seditions, heresies, envyings,* and *murders.* Then there are the ones that cause us to sin against ourselves: *drunkenness and revellings.* All of these sins fall under the heading of **"lust of the flesh, lust of the eye and the pride of life."** (1Jn 2:16)

Only seventeen works of the flesh are mentioned in the Bible (because the true number is too many to list). But I rejoice in *Knowing* that it only takes the seven elements that comprise the "fruit of the Spirit" to overcome them all!

Gal 5:22 But the fruit of the Spirit is love, joy, peace, longsuffering, gentleness, goodness, faith,

Gal 5:23 Meekness, temperance:

It is important to note that the "**works** of the flesh" are mentioned in a plurality but the fruit of the Spirit is mentioned in the context of one group that is comprised of seven components. The works of the flesh are usually accomplished by more than one demon spirit. If the Devil has decided to orchestrate a murder, the spirits that influence toward hatred may work with spirits that incite to wrath and strife and they may together work with the spirits that cause envyings and they may all work toward the primary assignment which is to push toward murder!

But it is the one Spirit of God that gives life and direction to the fruit of the Spirit. Realize this, Precious Heart, "Love does not need peace to enable love to do its work for love can work even in the heart that is in turmoil." And peace doesn't need joy for it to prevail because peace is a standalone authority of the Holy Spirit. Paul promises the people ". . . **And the peace of God, which passeth** all understanding, shall keep your hearts and minds through Christ Jesus." (Phil. 4:7)

". . . *a peace that passeth all understanding!* Joy is a source of strength in and of itself so the work of joy is not dependant on gentleness to pave the way for it. "What of longsuffering," you might ask. The durability and stamina of longsuffering can be in effect even if goodness doesn't show up! While true faith will overcome all obstacles and take on all comers and never falter or faint!

. . . against such there is no law.(Gal. 5:23b)

There are no restrictions, regulations, legally or otherwise to constrain or govern the proper use of the "fruit of the Spirit." There is literally nothing that can condemn this divine fruit! Actually, the closer one is to the Lord, the greater the use, value and appreciation of the fruit of the Spirit.

Rom 12:2 **And be not conformed to this world: but be ye transformed by the renewing of your mind, that ye may prove what** *is* **that good, and acceptable, and perfect, will of God.**

A man may feel the greatest comfort and have the strongest sense of self when he is wearing a flannel shirt, denim coveralls and a pair of well worn and broken-in brogan boots. But if that man desires to re-present himself to others in a more formal and classic look, he may have a tailor to custom make a tuxedo suit, a tuxedo shirt and buy a pair of dress shoes. After the new attire is purchased and delivered to the man—he cannot re-present himself as the dapper fellow that is his intention *until he puts the new clothing on!*

Similarly, the **"New Man"** was created by God and in God and was paid for by the blood of Jesus. But every soul that is **"transformed by the renewing of** . . . (the) . . . **mind"** still must **"put on"** the New Man!" For the New man needs the renewed mind in order for the New Man to have the thoughts and inclinations to do the Will of the Father. The Old Man (the natural man) **"**. . . <u>**receiveth not the things of the Spirit of God**</u>**: for they are foolishness unto him: neither can he know** *them,* **because they are spiritually discerned.** (Co 2:14)

The soul is not changed in its essence when a person is saved and sanctified—*there is simply a renewing of the mind.* Similarly, a person "puts off the old man" and is renewed in the spirit of his mind so that when he puts on the new man, he has a governor that will operate according to the Mind and the Will of God! That is the reason that the Apostle, Paul admonishes the Church to ". . . **be not conformed to this world: but be ye transformed by the renewing of your mind, that ye may prove what** *is* **that good, and acceptable, and perfect, will of God.** (Rom 12:2) What he is literally saying is, "Don't allow yourself to be molded by the worldliness of the world with its political correctness that accepts things that the Holy Spirit has rejected while saying to things that God has determined to be wrong, **"Be thou right!"** Rather, allow the perfection of the Almighty to be your standard of acceptability! *Receive from God* and *develop in God* so that your proclivities, inclinations and dispositions will be *new!* Change until the new things that you approve and disapprove will contradict the choices of the Old Man! Change until your understanding is enlightened and your compassion and concern for others stretches beyond the pale of what the Old Man would have cared for! Dear one, you must so embrace the mind of Christ that His Loves are your loves and things that incur His antipathies, aversions and hostilities are the very things that you hate and are in extreme opposition to!

"Put on the new man which after God is created in Righteousness and true Holiness." The template or the pattern of the new man is fashioned after the character of God Himself! Remember, Saints, from the beginning of His creation—God has used Himself as the flawless and unimpeachable Model of Perfection! When God made all things, He compared the quality of goodness and the faultless excellence of His creation with His Own characteristic attributes of exquisite perfectness and declared that all was *"good!"*

Thus, the end result of being ". . . **transformed by the renewing of your mind** . . ." and putting ". . . **on the new man** . . ." is ". . . **that ye may prove what** *is* **that good, and acceptable, and perfect, will of God."** (Rom. 12:2)

A Feather from the Eagle's Wings

You can only live in God to the extent that God lives in you!

CHAPTER 12

A SURPRISE WORTH WAITING FOR!

A Key Hint of the Exquisite Wonder of the Great Surprise

What we are dealing with here is the Imagination of God!

Cor. 2:9 **But as it is written, Eye hath not seen, nor ear heard, neither have entered into the heart of man, the things which God hath prepared for them that love him.**

There are things that the Father has chosen to be kept clothed in mystery and hidden from the attention of unworthy man. The date and time of His soon appearing is one of them. The true quality of life with all of the accoutrements and accessories that the rewarded believer will enjoy is another one. In man's wildest imaginings he has never and could never see, hear or hope for those things that that are created in the mind of God; things that transcend all that humankind believe are possible and even things that are so far removed from the mental and physical experiences of mankind that man has never even dreamed of them. In the Heart of the all Knowing God there are things that God has especially designed to be awarded to His faithful ones that are very literally *from out of this world!*

We expect and anticipate or expect and dread the things that we do because we have a frame of reference in our mind for believing those things to be good for us or bad for us! Depending on the appetite that we have for the thing that is desired *or the thing we fear*—we wait for it with the attitude that is appropriate to the expectation. However, when it comes to the promise of Heaven and all of its Wonders the only reference to go on is the understanding that the Designer and the Rewarder is the God of all Creation! So, it is truly with wide wonder that we gaze in our mind seeking to fathom and reason what the joys of Heaven will be! And because in our *Knowing* we perceive that God is a God of balance, we conclude that **as terrible as Hell will be,** where the **"worm dieth not,** (see Mark 9:44) *so exquisitely splendid and wondrous shall Heaven be!*

What we are dealing with here is the Imagination of God (actually, God doesn't have imagination—HE IS IMAGINATION! How can finite little man with his finite little mind ever hope to understand the Intelligence of the All Knowing One? **"O the depth of the riches both of the wisdom and knowledge of God! how unsearchable *are* his judgments, and his ways past finding out!"** (Rom 11:33) Remember, dear Reader, that man cannot comprehend the mind of God

"Because the foolishness of God is wiser than men." (1Co 1:25) We should not be at all surprised that **"Eye hath not seen, nor ear heard, neither have entered into the heart of man, the things which God hath prepared for them that love him."** Cor. 2:9

But wait a minute before we go on! **". . . the foolishness of God is wiser than men."** (1Co 1:25) One day when I was studying this verse of scripture, I asked the Lord what was meant by that statement. He said to me, "Son, My Wisdom is so far advanced over the wisdom of humanity that if I told you a joke, I would be doubled over laughing at the punch line and you would be standing there, scratching your head and saying, "Huh?"

"Lo, this is our God, we have waited for him, and he will save us: this is the Lord; we have waited for him, we will be glad and rejoice in his salvation." Isa. 25:9. *KJV*

There is no greater and more profound evidence of your faith than you quietly waiting with an unwavering expectation for Him while *knowing* that He can only keep His Word! He can do nothing less than keep His promise! **"It's All in The Knowing!"**

Only those who truly love Him will wait on Him because there are so many distractions in this world.

"Life and immortality are brought to light through the gospel." (2Tim 1:10)

Everything that is of this Earth is temporal, that is to say it has an expiration date. And though everything that is of

Earth was created and made by the Eternal God, nothing He made can exist forever because of father Adam's sin in the Garden of Eden and the subsequent curses God placed in the Earth.

If the things that God has prepared for those who love Him were of the earth and of the senses, human eyes and understanding could perceive and understand them but all that comes with *"Life and immortality ..."* are spiritual and are only revealed *"... through the gospel"* by *The Knowing ; the revelation!*

"But the natural man receiveth not the things of the Spirit of God: for they are foolishness unto him: neither can he know *them,* because they are spiritually discerned." (1Co 2:14)

The natural (the fleshly) man is all too often found lacking in patience! He is usually not willing to wait for much and when it comes to spiritual benefits the natural man's attention span is much too short! But the overall problem is not the attention span *but the natural man's inability to see the value in things that are spiritual.* It is his carnal knowledge; his greed and his selfishness that causes him to be so impatient. His carnal knowledge does not lend itself to him receiving the things of God because he is *"too wise"* (said sarcastically) to celebrate the goodness and honesty of simple and profound truths!

"In that hour Jesus rejoiced in spirit, and said, I thank thee, O Father, Lord of heaven and earth, that thou hast hid these things from the wise and prudent, and hast revealed them unto babes: even so, Father; for

so it seemed good in thy sight." (Luke 10:21) It is in part the makeup of the natural man to label those things "foolish" which his carnal understand cannot comprehend. For, often, he will not say that his knowledge is lacking in spiritual things. So, because he cannot admit that he does not know—HE CANNOT LEARN! If he cannot learn—HE CANNOT BECOME *what the truth would have made him!* I have said it before and I will say it again, *"Flesh gets man into trouble and his pride keeps him there!"*

CHAPTER 13

——⟫•◦⟪——

PUT OFF, RENEW AND PUT ON!

A Key to the "Why?" of Spiritual Weakness

*They really were saved **but their flesh was not!***

Col 3:9 . . . ye have put off the old man with his deeds;

Pews in the church are filled with folk who suppose that coming to Christ was the extent of their responsibilities as far as qualifying for the Rapture is concerned. They errantly enter their new spiritual life with the idea of just enjoying their salvation. Many are totally unaware that Satan is not finished with them yet and neither will he ever be done with them as long as they live and breathe on this earth. When they first were saved and perhaps for some time after that—**they lived an anointed and an inspired life.** They were not hearing the negatives that the "gainsayers" were saying about them. They were by no means cognizant of any lies or gossip that was going on about them. They were so heavenly that earth had little influence on their attitude. Every day was "Sunday" and praises were never far from their lips. But as time ensued they came down to earth and had to deal with the things of life. It was then that they began to feel the scrapes and scratches, bumps and bruises of life. Before they knew it they were dealing with the same bothersome things that troubled them before they were saved.

They really were saved but their flesh was not! So when they were adversely affected by the world around them they began to react in the same way that they used to before their conversion! Inwardly they were committed to live a life that their flesh was not about to agree with! But they found themselves reeling and rocking from the same things that they overcame them in their former life.

The responsibility for either living with the **"old man"** or getting rid of him rests directly on the shoulders of each soul! How do you **"put off"** that which not only is a part of you—it is actually you without the influence of God! It is you in the raw! It is you at your most basic self! How do you divest yourself of your own essence? What is there that shows you in such stark contrast *to who you were not?* What is there that spurred you, goaded you and compelled you to absolutely condemn that part of you that at one time was all of you! How did you come from loving yourself (your flesh) in a most unhealthy way to a point of self loathing yourself (your "old man") in a positive way?

The **"old man"** doesn't come empty! He is accompanied by his potentials, his desires, his weaknesses and his attitudes! These produce **"his deeds.** A truth that I have taught for years is, **"Your thoughts will become your actions; your actions will become your habits; your**

habits will become your character and your character is who you are!" It all starts with the thought! When the thought goes unchecked, actions follow and if done often and long enough the actions will become habits that will result in a change in character which will require that you do something! That is if you want to be approved by the Righteousness of God! Remember, **"For, as he thinketh in his heart, so *is* he."** (Pro 23:7)

So, the Old Man must be put off! Not only is the Old Man cursed by *The Knowing* but **the deeds** of the Old Man are **"put off"** as well! Both the Old Man and his deeds are to be **"put off,"** cast away!

In Luke 5:37, **Jesus said, "And no man putteth new wine into old bottles; else the new wine will burst the bottles, and be spilled, and the bottles shall perish."** There is a total incompatibility between the new wine which must go through a stringent process of fermentation and the old bottle (leather wineskin). The process of fermentation will surely eat away at the leather wineskin until the wineskin is completely destroyed. Similarly, the *"new man"* could not be simply put on **over** the **"old man!"** The differences are too stark, discordant and contradictory! The acidic and corrosive effects of the weights, sins and warrings of the flesh will cause a break down and absolute deterioration of the new man.

Consider that the Lord admonished Aaron to **"put difference between holy and unholy, and between unclean and clean. (**Lev 10:10)

Don't forget that Simon the Sorcerer tried to buy the power to lay hands on people to make them receive the Holy Ghost. **"But Peter said unto him, Thy money perish with thee, because thou hast thought that the gift of God may be purchased with money. Acts 8:20**

Act 8:21 Thou hast neither part nor lot in this matter: for <u>thy heart is not right in the sight of God.</u>

Act 8:22 Repent therefore of this thy wickedness, and pray God, if perhaps the thought of thine heart may be forgiven thee.

Act 8:23 For I perceive that <u>thou art in the gall of bitterness, and *in* the bond of iniquity.</u>"

As Simon's *<u>heart was</u>* in the sight of God—**so was Simon** in the sight of God! Sin cannot be dressed up and made presentable to God! One must actually **"<u>put off the old man </u>with his deeds"** and **"put on the new man!"**

Col 3:10 And have put on the new *man*, which is renewed in knowledge after the image of him that created him:

It is only after coming to *know God* that you can truly come to *know* who and what you are! Only as the creature comes to *know* the perfection of the Creator does the created see how imperfect a creature he is and how perfect he can become! And it is a natural course of action for the thing that was created to long for, yearn for and determine to become again—the image of his Creator!

When you **"put on"** the new man, you do not just redress yourself! You do not merely change spiritual attire! You have become a **"new creature"** (a new creation) with a new relationship with God, new strengths, and new potentials. You are no longer locked in to becoming the product of your earthly birth! The generational curses that have hounded and plagued your family can not touch you! **Therefore if any man *be* in Christ, *he is* a new creature: old things are passed away; behold, all things are become new.** (2Co 5:17) You were born again! But you have to put on the new man! That is why the Apostle, to the Gentiles, Paul, instructed the church to ". . . be not conformed to this world: but be ye transformed by the renewing of your mind, that ye may prove what *is* that good, and acceptable, and perfect, will of God."** (Rom. 12:2) Another thing that I want to point out is that we need to look at the word, **"renewing"** and understand that for the lessons in this book it means the same as the word, "Re-*knowing*!" All of the truths that Adam received from God are there waiting for the Sons of God to come into the knowledge of them! We are not to be as the people that Paul told Timothy about who are **"Ever learning, and never able to come to the knowledge of the truth. (2Ti 3:7)** It really is All in The Knowing!

Ever be aware that after your salvation *you retained* the weaknesses and proclivities of the flesh—*you have to exercise your power of choice* and put on the new man!

". . . Which is renewed in knowledge after the image of him that created him."

I love the fact that the new man is **"is <u>renewed in knowledge after the image of him that created him</u>.** That there is a need for renewal is abundantly evident! The question remains though, as to what the new standard of approval and acceptability will be! What will be used as the prototype! The only standard that the Perfect can accept is perfection! So God did as He did in the genesis of all things! Everything He made He evaluated and gave His sanction and endorsement by finding that it "... **was good.**" (Gen. 1:31) The only example of perfection that God had was His Own Perfect Self! I have often taught that *"your finished product is a signature of your character!"* Now, as long as you have not announced that you are finished with a project there is no need for an excuse as to why there are faults in the work! But as soon as you say, "I'm finished!" everyone will know whether you are a perfectionist or not! Few people will give you the benefit of the doubt and pardon your mistakes! Most will not say, "He did the best he could! They will simply conclude that He is "sorry!"

So, when God had to appraise His handiwork, He looked at His creation and then looked at His Own Perfection and saw a mirror image of His perfection in His workmanship. He, then, pronounced that "... **it was very good!**" (Gen. 1:31)

Feathers From the Eagle's Wings

THE OLD MAN IS PERFECTLY WILLING TO LIVE IN GOD'S PERMISSIVE WILL! THE NEW MAN ONLY DESIRES TO LIVE IN GOD'S PERFECT WILL—PERFECTLY!

CHAPTER 14

TO RENEW IS TO "RE-KNOW"

A Key to Man's Hope for this Chapter

". . . man was not set up for eternal failure!"

The new man is vested in the mind that was also in Christ Jesus! To "renew" the mind is actually to replace the old—*"Knowing!"* To "re-*know*" is to come back to the knowledge that Adam had before he sinned and was cursed! Adam's unlimited understanding and mental state was rendered most limited after he sinned and God cursed him and separated him from God! Adam made the worse trade in the history of man when He traded the mind that God gave him in creation for the "Knowledge of Good and Evil!" The New Man is renewed with the mind that man lost in the sin of Adam! The New Man loves what his Creator loves and can hear and receive what the Holy Spirit says to the Church! Adam could converse with the *"Voice of the Lord, God* "as He walked *"in the cool of the day."* (Gen 3:8) So, the more we put on the New Man the more we will be able to understand and receive the things of God!

After Adam's transgression, man is born with but a weak imitation of the mind that Adam was created with. And that mind is an almost grotesque caricature of the genius and the holiness of Adam's mind! Just to make this point, please be reminded that Adam was instructed by God to name all creatures. *(See Gen.2:19-20)* How many species and sub species of animals, insects and the like are there? Adam had to not only name them but remember their names as well so that he didn't name any two creatures the same name. How powerful and large would the computer have to be to do that today? Adam had no computer! All he had was his mind!

And how about this thought? **And they heard the voice of the LORD God walking in the garden in the cool of the day.** (Gen 3:8) It stands to reason that the Lord, God, was a frequent visitor in the Garden of Eden because when **"they heard the voice of the LORD God walking in the garden in the cool of the day,"** Adam and Eve recognized Him! They KNEW Him! The question should be asked, "When God came to talk to Adam—what did they talk about? Did they only talk about things that were shallow, finite and basic or were they able to talk about things that were on God's mind! Adam was made "in God's image!" He was both spiritual and natural! That part of him that was natural was natural but that part of him that was spiritual was all spiritual! That is why God was able to entrust man with having dominion over the earth!

Man lost so much more than most people know when Adam sinned! When Adam sinned—man lost his innocence! He was filled with earthly wisdom and sophistication! But he also lost—*The Knowing!* Yes! He lost the relationship that he had with God! He lost the oneness that he had enjoyed and the intimacy that he had with his Creator! And he lost the privilege of living in Eden!

But all is not lost! There is hope after all! There is a way out! As bleak as the picture of man's outlook seems to be *man was not set up for eternal failure!* For, remember God's entire intent when he made man! Gen 1:26 **And God said, Let us make man <u>in our image</u>, <u>after our likeness</u>.** God wanted man to be in the image of God! So that is how God made man—in His Own image! But what about Joh 4:24, Jesus said, **"<u>God *is* a Spirit</u>: and they that worship him must worship *him* in spirit and in truth."** And be reminded that Jesus told Thomas, **"Behold my hands and my feet, that it is I myself: handle me, and see; for <u>a spirit hath not flesh and bones,</u> as ye see me have."** (Luke 24:39) Now, we know that man has flesh and bones! But we also know that a spirit doesn't!

So, the job here is twofold. Man is to be made **"<u>In the image of God</u>"** and man is to be made **"<u>after his likeness!</u>"** Well, how was that to be done? But before I answer that question let me pose another one. The Word said, **"And God said, Let <u>us </u>make man in our image, after our likeness."** But in verse 27, when it was recorded who made man it says, **So God created man in <u>his *own* image,</u> in the image of God created <u>he </u>him; male and female created <u>he </u>them.** (Gen 1:27) Now, we know that the Word says, "Let us make man but when the Word of God says who made man the word said, "**God created man in <u>his *own* image</u>." In the image of God created HE him; male and female created HE them!** Well, those who have **The Knowing** (the spirit of revelation) will see that the Father created man in His image. According to Strong's #OT:6755 the word, "image" is translated from tselem (tseh'-lem); from an unused root meaning to shade; a phantom, i.e. (figuratively) illusion, resemblance; hence, a representative figure, especially an idol. KJV—image, vain shew.

Please note that the words that come into play are the words, "resemblance," a "representative figure" and "image." All of these words speak of the ability to cause something to be made like something else. To "resemble" is to look or be like something. A "representative figure" must have something in common with that which is represented and an "image" must have its origin in something other than itself.

The word image is the root of the word, "imagination." So it was God Who imagined what man would look like! That we have two arms and two legs with a head having two eyes one nose and a mouth—IS GOD'S IMAGE OF WHAT A MAN WOULD LOOK LIKE! That took care of man being made **in the image of God!**

Look! If you are an architect and you design a house that you imagined—that house would be made in your image! For, you would surely copyright or patent the design. So, every house that was made according to that design would be made in your image because you own the image! It came out of you and from you! It is your image! So, we are made in the image that God thought up! The human form is God's image so all humankind is made in the image of God because the image of the human form is God's image!

But, what about making us **after the likeness**? The promise was that man would be made **"after our likeness"** or in God's *resemblance* and as a *"representative figure"* of God. So, what is God *like* and to **Whom** was God speaking? The answer is simple though very profound! God was talking down the line of time to the Word that was made flesh—the Son, Jesus! *God is Holy!* And just as it was the Father's responsibility to give us our physicality (our human body) so it was the Son's job to give us our spirituality; our holiness—the likeness of God! Contemplate this: Gen. 1:26 **And God said, "Let us make man in our image, after our likeness: and let <u>them have dominion over</u> the fish of the sea, and over the fowl of the air, and over the cattle, and over all the earth, and <u>over every creeping thing that creepeth upon the earth."</u>**

Gen 1:27 **So, God created man in his *own* image, in the image of God created he him; male and female created he them.**

Gen 1:28 **And God blessed them, and God said unto them, "Be fruitful, and multiply, and replenish the earth, and subdue it: and <u>have dominion over</u> the fish of the sea, and over the fowl of the air, <u>and over every living thing that moveth upon the earth."</u>**

eBISHOP J. A. TOLBERT 1ST

This proves that Adam was designed to use his entire brain—not the small percentage that most people use today! But when Adam sinned, man also lost his ability to think like God intended man to think! God wanted man to be just like Him on this earth; to lord over it and to have dominion over it—but do it in loving kindness and tender mercies! However, because of sinful Adam, man lost his ability to use his lordship as God would use it! He did not lose power but he did lose control (self control)! God never wanted to use His muscle and His authority to control man—NO! God wanted to inspire man through his anointed Word! God wanted to lead men as shepherds lead their sheep! But gone were man's innocence and his gentleness! Gone were his surrender and his obedience! Gone were his gratitude and his devotion! God's masterpiece has become His greatest failure! His Centerpiece has become His greatest sorrow! *NOT THAT GOD FAILED MAN BUT THAT MAN FAILED GOD!*

Man now could be brutal, destructive and controlling! He had lost the kind of respect for himself, his power and his compassion that His Creator and his Mentor wanted him to have. God never intended that man conquer man! He never intended that man subjugate his brothers and make slaves of them. But, tragically, God knew what man would become when he sinned!

Feathers from the Eagle's Wings

The tongue doesn't have a brain—the brain has a tongue!

CHAPTER 15

THE "BEST" IS IN THE KNOWING!

A Key to Paul's Success in this Chapter

"One born out of due time—is one born just in time!"

There is a story that I heard many years ago. I don't remember exactly just how the story goes but I do remember the point of the story. So, I will make up my own story to illustrate a point and perhaps, share a knowledge.

One day in a land far away, an old beggar man sat at the side of a road asking for anything of value that passersby would give him. As he sat there, a very fine carriage pulled by a brace of four splendid horses drove up. The young prince told his driver to stop the carriage and when the coach came to a halt the young prince called the old man over to him. With a great grunt of effort the old man got to his feet and approached the carriage. The very wealthy young prince had compassion on the beggar and held his hand out toward the old man. Between his thumb and his forefinger he held an object which he offered the old beggar.

"Old, man," the young prince began, "This ring is the best of all of my treasures. It is so valuable that it is truly priceless! If you will sell this ring wisely—you will never have to beg again for the rest of your life!"

With quivering and shaking hands the old man reached up to receive the offering. He could scarcely believe his eyes for, before him was the most exquisite ring he had ever seen! The diamonds seem to dance with the shining of a thousand lights each more beautiful and wondrous than the others! The scarlet rubies shone with the very fire of the sun. And the deep blue sapphires gleamed with the dark blue depths of a million midnights! Truly this was the grandest, most magnificent gift that anyone had ever received in all of history!

"Sir," the old man ventured to say, "I don't know how I can ever thank you for so wonderful a gift! But the young prince simply waved away any further words of gratitude and shouted up to his driver, "Be off now, driver!"

In a great cloud of dust the carriage rushed away and around the bend of the road out of the old man's sight! Amid the settling dust, the old man held the ring up close to his eyes and squinted to take in all of its singular and unique beauty. Then, instead of putting the ring on his finger, the old man did a very curious thing. He packed the ring away in the bottom of the old bag that held all of his worldly possessions. The old beggar then tucked the bag under his arm, adjusted his walking stick so that he could move a little faster and hurried through the remaining dust in the direction the fine carriage had gone.

Two days later the old man arrived at the palace of the rich young prince who had blessed him with the most exquisite diamond ring. He pulled on the great gold rope that hung down beside one of the huge ornately carved double doors! Soon, the door was opened by a beautifully attired servant who graciously asked, "Can I be of service to you, sir?" The old man was astonished at this so cordial a greeting because all of his life he had been chased, rejected and cursed! The old man knew that the master of this house was indeed an exceptional person.

"Why, yes, you can!" he replied. He reached into his bag to the very bottom and drew out the ring and handed it to the servant. The servant, having seen it many times, asked harshly, "Where did you get this ring! It belongs to my master!" The old man shrank back in fear and quickly protested, "I didn't steal it! Your master gave it to me when I was begging! Before the servant could answer, the old man continued, "Please, will you take this ring to him so that he will know who it is that is asking to speak with him?"

The servant, with a look of doubt and accusation took the ring, closed the door and went back inside the palace. When he offered the ring to the young prince, the young man took the ring and with much anger in his voice, said, "I will not see this old man! What more can he want? I gave him my best! If my best did not satisfy him,—I HAVE NOTHING BETTER TO GIVE!" As the servant walked away to go and tell the old man the young prince's word, the prince had a change of mind.

"Wait!" He commanded his servant. "I will see him! I want to see just how greedy and ungrateful that old beggar can be!" So the servant went out to get the old man.

The Prince will see you now," he informed the beggar. "Please follow me." He led the old man down a great hall that had a very high ceiling and walls that were adorned with portraits of all of the royalty that had ever lived in the great palace! When they came to the end of the hall they turned right into the library where the Prince had been reading.

At the sound of their footsteps the Prince turned to face them. "What, Old Man, could you possibly be here to ask of me? I told you when I gave you the ring that I had given you my best! Why could you not have been satisfied with the ring? Because you are so greedy and unappreciative I will now take back the ring I so willing gave you! Now what have you to say?"

The old man was so ashamed that he had angered the young Prince that he could hardly look up at him. Looking down at his bare feet and the ragged and frayed ends of his pants legs, the old man whispered, "Sir, I am most grateful to you for the gift you gave me. I am not here because I did not appreciate the ring. It is a better gift than I have ever received in my life and better than I had ever hoped to receive! But I must confess that you do have something that is infinitely more valuable than the ring!" The young prince looked at him both sternly and questioningly. "What can you possible think that I have that is greater in value than the ring I gave you?" he demanded.

The old man lifted his head high for the first time in the presence of the rich young Prince and answered, "That which I treasure more than the priceless ring you gave me is the quality of love in your heart that made you give me such a priceless gift! That love is what I want!"

The Apostle, Paul had a similar experience with God when he desired, **"That I may know him, and the power of his resurrection, and the fellowship of his sufferings, being made conformable unto his death." (Php 3:10)** Paul had to think himself to be the most blessed man he knew! He had received to his benefit, the death, burial and the resurrection of the Lord, Jesus Christ! He had further, received such an abundance of *knowing* that he needed to have the messenger of Satan (a thorn in his side to buffet him) less he be lifted up (in pride) because of his revelations. Though he was as **"one born out of due time,"** Paul saw Jesus at the last before He ascended from this earth to heaven. Keep in mind that he felt that he was ". . . **not meet to be called an apostle, because I persecuted the church of God. But by the grace of God I am what I am: and his grace which *was bestowed* upon me was not in vain** (1Co 15:8-10)

Despite this, however, the Apostle was not satisfied to be the beneficiary of the Plan of Salvation and of the Lord's immeasurable Love! He appreciated to the max the fact that he was saved; that he was sanctified and filled with the Holy Ghost but he was just as adamant about *knowing*, feeling and experiencing the changing Power of His resurrection! As well, he had a dire need to know by a "fellowship" *(Grk. 2842: partnership, social intercourse, participation, fellowship)* the suffering that Jesus endured. He yearned to do more than stand at a distance and imagine the torture, pain and ultimately the death of his Lord. Paul wanted to know by experience, the price that was paid for his salvation. He wanted to know what it cost to lift him out of the bottomless quagmire of sin that was deservedly—his birthplace, his world and his destiny! Paul had some semblance of an idea of the cost of his salvation and his relationship with Christ (meaning the Crucifixion). But he wanted as well to know the price that was paid to raise him up to "newness of life." And what was the charge for his being made conformable unto the death of Christ? He realized that though many people were crucified—it would take a miracle for anybody to be crucified like Christ; to be reckoned like That Crucified One! He did not want merely to vicariously accompany Jesus to the Cross. Paul wanted to be *one with* our Lord in sanctification! For, that was the purpose of the death, burial and resurrection of the Lord! Our Sanctification! To be made conformable to his death is to be made conformable *to the reason for His death*; is to be sanctified! As long as we are clothed in our *"old man"* and until we have **"put on Christ"**—we are not conformed to His death! Until we are **"crucified with Him,"** having reckoned ourselves dead and having mortified the deeds of the flesh—we are not made conformable to His death! Only when the world is crucified in us by the Power of the work done at Calvary—HAVE WE CONFORMED UNTO HIS DEATH!

It is All About The Knowing! "... that I might know **Him**!" To know the Power of His resurrection is to know that I can be resurrected! To know the fellowship of His sufferings is to know *how* and *that* you can suffer for and in Him!

A Feather from the Eagle's Wings

"Because God is love He never has to decide to love but He does have to decide not to love!"

CHAPTER 16

PATIENCE POWER

A Key to Becoming the Product of Patience is in this Chapter

Her influence, will and purpose will be felt by all who don't hinder in her divine mission!

For ye have need of patience, that, after ye have done the will of God, ye might receive the promise. (Heb. 10:36)

We live in a world that is characterized by the desire for instant gratification. Everyone seems to be in a hurry. People seem to be more "want" driven than "necessity" driven. "I want it now!" they declare. Additionally, many people spell "want"—"NEED!" However, many times God doesn't work instantaneously. Oft times, there is process that must be respected. Jesus stated in Luke 21:19, **"In your patience possess ye your souls."** Whether the delay is the result of a process at work or simply God's timing—*patience is often the order of the day!*

At some point in time (I pray that it is sooner rather than later) the Saints of God have to get a *Knowing* in their spirit that says, *"Patience is not always passive!"* *There are times when patience will wear down the obstruction and make room for the desirable!*

Note that the learned Apostle, James admonished the Church to ". . . **let patience have *her* perfect work, that ye may be perfect and entire, wanting nothing.** (Jas 1:4) James speaks of patience as if "she" is a living thing that has influence, will and purpose! And, indeed she is all and has all of that! Truly, the Patience that is not diluted with any alloy of a weak character is a living entity that does have influence, will and purpose! **She even has a job!** And she is expected (if she is allowed) to do PERFECT WORK! Her influence, will and purpose will be felt by all who don't hinder in her divine mission! If there is one thing that the Child of God must do it is—*stay out of Patience's way!* She knows what she is doing! She has been doing it for a long time now! Trust her! Believe in her! *It is only because Patience is assured of victory that she never hurries!* Slow down and keep pace with Patience! Don't doubt her when you don't see any activity or change! She is able to do PERFECT WORK and all who will love her, honor, her and protect her WILL BE MADE PERFECT! *Know* this!

Precious heart, you must fight to retain and maintain your *Knowing* about Patience! You owe it to the God of your Patience! You owe it to the Patience of your God! And you owe it to yourself to *Know* the Power of Patience!

In Habakkuk 2:3, God's will is for His people to wait **"For the vision is yet for an appointed time, but at the**

end it shall speak, and not lie: though it tarry, wait for it because it will surely come, it will not tarry." The Apostle, Paul reasons, *"But if we hope for that we see not, then do we with patience wait for it. (Rom. 8:25)*

What is the basis for Patience Power? What is the foundation for one becoming a "Waiting Wonder?" *What is the active ingredient for one gladly waiting for that which has no deadline?* How could Abraham, ". . . **who is the father of us all** . . ." (Rom. 4:16) believe God (to have children) despite the reality of his body being ". . . **now dead when he was about an hundred years old . . . ?**" And how did he ignore ". . . **the deadness of Sara's womb?**"

Isn't it so like the Mind of the Omniscient God to condemn and utter the sentence of death over the vehicle by which blessings are to flow to His own beloved Saints? Indeed, ". . . **as the heavens are higher than the earth, so are my ways higher than your ways, and my thoughts than your thoughts.**" (Isa. 55:9) KJV And He has been known to threaten not only the blessing but the methods by which the blessing is to produce itself. For example, Jesus, the Savior of the world entered the world, lived in the world and then *He died in the world in the most ignoble way!* He was born in a lowly bacteria infested, dusty and smelly stable of an unwed mother! Then He lived the life of the itinerate preacher and vagabond Who was destined to become "Public Enemy #1! And was crucified by the same people He came to deliver and save. Further, the only way His devotees could follow Him was they had to forfeit all they had and do it based on a bunch of promises. No wonder some said of Him as He hang on the cross, *"He saved others; himself he cannot save."* (Matt. 27:42)

Feathers from the Eagle's Wings

"God cannot leave anywhere because there is nowhere for Him to go that He is not!"

CHAPTER 17

———⟫•⟨———

HOPE IS IN THE *"KNOWING!"*

A Key to Knowing Where Abraham's Hope was is in this Chapter

Abraham's hope was in his "Knowing!" His Joy was in his "Knowing!" His victory was in his "Knowing!"

All spiritual answers lie in *"The Knowing!"* Oh! What a profound truth Jesus spoke when He taught, **"And ye shall know the truth, and the truth shall make you free."** (John 8:32) It is not simply truth that makes one free. It is *the truth that one knows* that *makes one free!* There is no truth that does not have power and potential to influence if one *Knows* the truth and how to use it! Even though he may never have used the word, Abraham knew that God's Word is "Immutable!" It cannot mutate, change or metamorphose! (See Heb. 6:18) It is forever settled in Heaven! (See Ps. 119:89)

(As it is written, I have made thee a father of many nations,) before him whom he believed, even God, who

quickeneth the dead, and calleth those things which be not as though they were. (Rom. 4:17)

"I have made thee a father of many nations."

Please note the past tense of the word, **"made."** Abraham _knew_ that when God speaks He sets in motion a law. He calls into existence a continuum. For instance, God said **"Let there be light"** only one time and there has been light on earth ever since! In essence, He very literally said, "Let there be **light,** light, light, light, ad infinitum! So, when God said **"I have made thee a father of many nations"** Abraham _knew_ that he was a father **before His wife knew she would conceived!** For Abraham _knew_ that God _"quickeneth the dead"_ _which means that God gives life to the dead! So_ **He could give life to her dead womb!** The "Father of Faith" **knew** that God ". . . **calleth those things which be not as though they were."** (Rom. 4:17) Abraham's hope was _in his "knowing"!_ His Joy was _in his "knowing"!_ His victory was _in his "knowing"!_

113

Feathers from the Eagle's Wings

The tongue's poison and evil is in its potential because the tongue can do nothing on its own! It must be ordered by the mind!

CHAPTER 18

————⊱•⊰————

PRUDENCE AND WISDOM VS. FAITH

The Key to Solving the great
Puzzle is in this *Chapter*

Man's Prudence and wisdom vs. Divine Declaration:
Who Wins?

Who against hope believed in hope, that he might become the father of many nations; according to that which was spoken, "So shall thy seed be." ROM. 4:16

Abraham, ". . . **against hope believed in hope** . . . ." The great puzzle here is that **despite the fact that God has declared what would be** and even though what God pronounces ***immediately*** becomes a law all over the universe, *if we would go by man's prudence and wisdom,* ***the only real hope is that which is presented by natural law and common sense!***

Abraham's one hundred years old body is dried up and Sarah's womb is dead! The only reasonable hope and expectancy is that not only will Abraham never be the "Father of Many Nations"—*he will never father <u>one</u> child!*

Quite often we find that there were those in the Bible who, by the Grace of God, found themselves partaking of a quality of spiritual Bread that few in their time had tasted. Hopeful people were not always scarce in the times of the Bible. Neither were believers always in great shortage. But here we find Abraham not being simply hopeful; neither is he just believing. For, to **hope deals** primarily **with** *"possibility"* while **belief** usually **has to do with** *"probability."*

In "hoping" one knows that a thing could happen but doesn't know that it will. Take for instance, the weather in the Sahara Desert. It *could* rain thirty-six inches there every day for a month. But because we know the climate in the Sahara Desert we also know that on any day there it is certain *to not rain thirty-six inches!*

On the other hand, one may know that given the variables that are present, it is more likely than not that a thing will occur. Continuing with the Sahara Desert analogy it is more likely than not that *the sun will shine* every day for a month. That happenstance is called, *"probable."* But concerning the fact that it is God Who uttered the decree that Abraham will be the father of many nations Abraham *knew* that his fatherhood was substantially more than "possible" but it is also infinitely more than "probable!" Abraham **KNEW** it was absolutely certain!

Feathers from the Eagle's Wings

Tomorrow you will become who you were becoming yesterday unless you change today!

CHAPTER 19

———◆———

THE FAITH EQUATION

A Key to How Abraham Produced Faith in this Chapter

*What Abraham hoped—when joined with what he believed—produced a **knowing!***

True faith in God is the result of implementing this equation:

The willingness to believe (hope)
\+ God's Integrity
\+ God's Power
————————————————
    Faith in God

It is totally impossible for reasonably thinking individuals to add these two elemental traits of the Sovereign God together properly and not have faith in Him! But to do this you have to KNOW GOD'S CHARACTER; HIS

POWER AND HIS PROMISE! *ITS ALL IN THE KNOWING!*

Abraham, "... **against hope believed in hope!**" There is no cause for the great patriarch to be alarmed for he has walked with God; has tried God and has witnessed, firsthand, God keeping His Word and fulfilling His Promises! So, for Abraham it's a "no brainer!" He married hope and belief together! He **"against hope—believed *in* hope!"** Abraham actually took his hope in God (possibility) and married it to his belief in God (probability)! What a recipe for a miracle! When Abraham added hope with belief he produced more than hope and belief! He produced **the certainty of success; he produced unfailing confidence in the Integrity of God** and he produced **a conviction concerning the inestimable, inexhaustible, Omnipotent strength of God!** Blended together, these properties produce that certainty of success hat is called, *"faith."* While hope says, **"It is possible,"** belief says, **"It's probable!"** And *faith* declares in a stentorian voice "It is actual! It is genuine! It is real! It exists! It is truth! *It's a done deal!*"

Abraham hoped to become a "father of many nations" and his hope—*when joined with what he believed*—produced a *knowing* that said, "Despite all evidences to the contrary—**I am a father!**" Abraham *Knew!*

Again, "hope" (a measure of faith) is the possibility that a thing can occur! Belief (a measure of faith) is the probability that brings forth actuality when the two are blended! Hope married to belief produces a faith that will activate the Integrity of God and His Integrity activates His Power and the result is answered prayer!

Feathers from the Eagle's Wings

Dear Jesus,

Please lead me today into the destiny you prepared me for yesterday so I can lead others tomorrow!

CHAPTER 20

———⟫•⟪———

HEAVEN'S WORD—THE FINAL ANSWER

A Key to What Abraham Knew that gave him his "Final Answer"

*"He **knew** that earth's realities could not prevent or thwart Heaven's agenda!"*

And being not weak in faith, he considered not his own body now dead, when he was about an hundred years old, neither yet the deadness of Sara's womb: (Rom. 4:19)

It may be said that "the height of (carnal) wisdom is to approach every obstacle logically." It is also the epitome and the essence of human weakness and frailty to *give undo consideration* to the hindrances that menace and threaten the credibility of a divine pledge or promise. Such **was not** the heart, mind and spirit of Abraham! He was not weak in faith!

For Abraham to "... **consider his** ..." dead ..." body and re-examine the situation would be to *reconsider Divine Wisdom* and *second guess the mind of God!* On what basis do men re-evaluate what God has sanction and ordained? If the All *Knowing* God ever could make a mistake—the finite mind of man would never detect it and certainly could never think beyond and above it to rectify it! Also, one of the reasons that God cannot make a mistake is that if He did make a mistake He would do it on purpose and then His mistake would be swallowed up by His success in purposefully making a mistake! So, Abraham never had the thought to re-think Divine Providence.

God's children must be clear about another thing also! Real faith does not ignore negative variables nor does it dismiss them. Rather, *true faith deals with them!* True faith can afford to take on all comers who would deny the truthfulness of faith! True faith does not cause true believers to say, "I don't receive that" when faced with negativity or "I don't believe that" when the report is unfavorable! The true believer receives and believes the true report but also looks to Heaven to see what the Lord has to say! Earth may have a "say" in the matter but Heaven has the "final say!"

Abraham was not weak in faith so he did not allow the negatives to have a viable voice in the matter. He had years of *Knowing* that his body was dead as was Sarah's but he also **_Knew_** that God could quicken (give life to) the dead! That being the case he **_Knew_** that earth's realities could not prevent or thwart Heaven's agenda!

Feather's from the eagle's Wings

Faith is: "believing that God will when the Devil says, "He won't!" My father again!

CHAPTER 21

FAITH FULL ONES DO NOT STAGGER

A Key to the reason people doubt God in this chapter

*When we stagger in the throes of confusion it is not because the promise of God failed—it is because **our faith was weighed in the balance and found wanting!***

He staggered not at the promise of God through unbelief; but was strong in faith, giving glory to God; Rom. 4:20

- A double minded man is unstable in all his ways. (James 1:8)

- Draw nigh to God, and he will draw nigh to you. Cleanse your hands, ye sinners; and purify your hearts, ye double minded. (James 4:8)

When people stagger at the promises of God they must come up with a "plan B." *They only have a "plan B" when* they don't trust the Mind and Heart of God to give or do for them what they want the most! These people are "double-minded" because *they want the Will of God **and** they want the desires of the flesh!*

But this is not to say that their hands and hearts are always filthy with the stains of overt sins of the flesh. Sometime the stains can only be seen through spiritual vision! And some of these people are "Church Folk; God's own!

Their **"staggering"** is clear indication that *their spiritual equilibrium is off!* They are no longer leaning squarely on the Rock of Ages! They depend on their many ideas, logics, feelings and desires that waver with their appetites, whims and changing situations! These are the reasons they must be commanded to **"draw nigh to God"** (Jas. 4:8) with the promise that God will not reject them but ". . . **will draw nigh to you.**"

Those who "stagger" do so because they have little or no stability. They find themselves at the mercy of each moment and every condition. When things seem to be going their way they are "up" and when the untoward occurs they are "down." The best thing that can be said for those who "stagger" is that they did not fall though they did falter! They did not quit though they did stumble! However, it may not be that they always stumbled in the right direction but as long as they did not give up or fall down—they had hope of success! Remember, my dear Reader, what staggering is! Staggering is a process of falling and catching oneself before hitting the ground! I don't want to glorify the notion of staggering but it takes more to stagger than it does to fall down! And please understand that staggering is a sign that one has not thrown in the towel of defeat! In order to "stagger," one has to use muscle power (mental, physical or emotional) to overcome a downward trajectory, or at the very least one has to win against the impetus and thrust of some influence that would pull one in a wrong direction. In any event, negative forces that would frustrate one's purposed agenda have to be defeated! Some people stagger because *they are not fully convicted to walk with God* but they also *are not surrendered completely to walk with Satan!* **So, they "stagger!"** They may not be full of doubt but they are not full of faith in God either. **So, they "stagger!"**

Yes! Those who are double minded are unstable in all their ways! But we know that Abraham did not stagger or falter because **he never had a plan "B!"** He never needed one! He never second guessed his Lord! He needed no second opinion! He didn't need to "mull it over!" As far as Abraham was concerned *when God made a promise it was a done deal! The Jury was in! The die was cast!* Abraham entertained no alternative to the Word of God; no option!

Abraham ". . . **staggered not at the promise of God through unbelief.**" There is no other reason to stagger at the promise of God than—unbelief! When we stagger in the throes of confusion, wonder and unbelief it is not because the promise of God failed—*it is because our faith was weighed in the balance <u>and found wanting!</u>*

Feathers from the Eagle's Wings

When you know that you are spiritually weak—make no major decisions!

CHAPTER 22

FOUR FORMS OF BELIEF

A Key to Knowing the "Fine Print" of *Unbelief and Disbelief*

"One cannot doubt the truthfulness of God's Word without calling God a liar."

1. Faith
2. Belief
3. Unbelief

Belief, trust and confidence in any form and to any degree of intensity and purity are influential forces because they have life. But these elements are not self sustaining because *they are reliant on a thinker*.

I know that Heb11:1 says, **"Now faith is the substance of things hoped for, the evidence of things not seen."** However, my father, the late former pastor, District Elder and Evangelist, Samuel D. Tolbert Sr. taught a very simple but profound definition of "faith." He taught that "faith is: *"believing that God will when the Devil says He won't!"*

The faith that is in the heart of the *"faither"* (to coin a word) has its origin in the very confidence that God has in Himself! Resident in the character of God is His Assurance and His Confidence in His Eternal and Omni—Self! The true believer's "faith" in God is actually the believer's *Knowing* at work! According to Paul's epistle to the Church in Rome, ". . . **faith** *cometh* **by hearing and hearing by the word of God."** (Rom 10:17) Now, **the Word of God—is "God!"** (See John 1:1) Therefore, it necessarily follows that God's *Knowing about* Himself *cannot be separated from Himself!* So, when God filled the Church with the Holy Spirit (Himself) **God filled the Church with the confidence and belief that He has in Himself!** When the confidence and trust that God has in Himself is found active in the Church—**that confidence and belief is called, *"faith!"*** That is one of the reasons that ". . . **without faith** *it is* **impossible to please** *him*." (Heb 11:6) If you don't present *faith* to **God <u>you deny God some of Himself and that will never please the Almighty!</u>**

It must be understood that the only things that please God are **those things that are <u>of</u> God!** The things that God approved in the genesis of all things and called them "good" and "very good," were *of, from* and *by* God! (See Genesis Chapter 1) The only ones of humankind that please God are ". . . **we** . . ." who ". . . **are <u>his workmanship</u>, created in Christ Jesus unto good works, which God hath before ordained that we should walk in them."** (Eph 2:10)

Belief suggests that something or someone *has been accepted as true* or *genuine* and belief often creates a confidence in that which is at issue. A very good analogy that clarifies the basic difference between faith and belief is the distinction between the standards of guilt in criminal case compared to the burden of proof and evidence in a small claims case. In the criminal case the standard is *"beyond a reasonable doubt"* whereas in a small claims case the measure of proof is *"a preponderance of the evidence."* In the former situation guilt must be proven by such a certainty of evidence that no reasonable person would refute! In the latter case the scales of proof have to be in balance so that *"it is more likely than not"* that the crime was committed by the accused. Belief says, "It's possible to the point of being probable" while faith declares the reality of the things in question. But belief is also more than willing to see the actual manifested!

When Jesus gave the formula for those who will qualify to be saved, He didn't implement a standard that was so stringent, inflexible and strict that a miracle of faith would be needed. He simply required that we *"believe!"* (Joh 3:16) **For God so loved the world, that he gave his only begotten Son, that whosoever believeth in him should not perish, but have everlasting life.** In Mat 21:22 we find, **And all things, whatsoever ye shall ask in prayer, believing, ye shall receive.** Concerning the existence of God, when the conclusion to the whole matter of what is possible is *"It is more likely than not"* that God exists, the result is—**not only does God exist**—a <u>**believer also exists!**</u>

Unbelief *is no belief at all!* It does not lean to either the positive or the negative! It is no more supportive of one aspect than it is another aspect. Unbelief has no allegiance to anything! Unbelief always leaves one confused not *knowing what, if anything is, right.* The great tragedy is that the unbeliever is denied the benefits and the rewards that are the entitlements of the believer. The unbeliever has no faith, no conviction and no confidence in anything! Consider the instructions Jesus gave to "doubting"Thomas, **"Then saith he to Thomas, Reach hither thy finger, and behold my hands; and reach hither thy hand, and thrust *it* into my side: and be not faithless, but believing.** (Joh 20:27) If Thomas had been allowed to continue in his suspicion he would have reasoned away the greatest boon and benefit to himself and to mankind since the world began! Don't miss the fact that Jesus commanded Thomas to ". . . **be not faithless, but believing.**" Jesus required Thomas to be rid of his faithlessness! Thomas was ordered to simply and purposefully step into the realm of belief! Nowhere does Jesus suggest that being a believer is a process. He does not tell Thomas to "become believer! He simply said, ". . . **be not faithless, but believing.**" This act of obedience simply required a willing heart and mind to do what the Son of God commanded. The command is twofold:

1. ". . . **be not faithless,**
2. **but believing.**"

Though all that was said about faith and belief is most certainly true, there are times when the Bible uses the words, "faith' and "belief" synonymously. From the context and by using a good translator one can recognize the differences.

Disbelief, on the other hand, *is a belief!* It is the very confident certainty *that something or somebody is not to be believed!* Disbelief is actually the "anti-faith." The strength of disbelief is such that it actually rivals, if not parallels, true faith because of its conviction and confidence. Disbelief is the heartbeat of the atheist! The true atheist is not in doubt about the non-existence of God! Rather, the true atheist is absolutely confident that there is no God! I remember a conversation that I had with my Psychology professor when he was trying to convince me that God does not exist. He stated his case with so much certainty and assurance that I commended him on the strength and quality of his faith! He rose up in his chair and declared, "I have no faith! How dared you say that I do!" I very calmly said that I wish that every Christian had his kind of faith; a faith that has no alloy of doubt and suspicion and is totally devoid of even a modicum of wavering. I mean, let's keep it real! Many, if not all, Christians have or will have their moment of doubt and uncertainty *about the existence of God!* But he had **no doubts** *about the non-existence of God!* I went on to explain to him that it is only by faith that he declares his atheistic views because he has no proof that can support his heresy. I further asserted that if he would choose to employ that faith in the positive—he would be one of the Church's staunchest and most powerful supporters!

Disbelievers rarely "stagger!" Unbelievers occasionally do! Disbelievers walk with a confidence that is almost a swagger. They go forth boldly; often with a bravado and will at times exude the quiet strength of a diehard conviction. The Devil will also brace the Disbeliever with the firm footing of arrogance and cockiness that is characteristic of a devilish devil-may-care attitude! Disbelief is actually the result of Satan poisoning the confused *unbeliever* with a satanic "dis-anointing" (to coin another word). The "dis-anointing" is actually the anti-power of Satan. The "anti-power" is the strength that enables disbelievers to sin with greater authority and conceive with an imagination that is more evil than the individual can employ on his/her own. Also, by the authority of the anti-power one can lust and desire to a greater degree than the human appetite can muster. Be reminded of the Apostle, Paul's admonition to the Church "**. . . that ye henceforth walk not as other Gentiles walk, in the vanity of their mind.**" (Eph. 4:17) "**Who being past feeling have given themselves over unto lasciviousness, to work all uncleanness with greediness.**" (Eph 4:19) **Lasciviousness,** defined as "unbridled lusts" or "lust without constraints. **Now the Spirit speaketh expressly, that in the latter times <u>some shall depart from the faith, giving heed to seducing spirits, and doctrines of devils;</u> (**1Ti 4:1) **Speaking lies in hypocrisy; <u>having their conscience seared with a hot iron;</u>** (1Ti 4:2) These realities are all produced by the *"anti-power"* of Satan!

When Satan gives life to views that are anti the mind of God—the result is a *"Disbeliever!"* The Devil's answer to *the believer* and the complete opposite of those who have faith is the *"Disbeliever!"*

It is a fact that unbelief can keep one off balance. Abraham "**<u>staggered</u> not at the promise of God <u>through unbelief</u>** . . . ." One cannot doubt the truthfulness of God's Word without calling God a liar and this Abraham would never do! The loss of spiritual equilibrium would never be a part of Abraham's life experiences because he was so

"strong in faith" that he **"staggered not at the promise of God through unbelief."**

Any strength of certainty that is found in a promise is inexorably linked to the integrity of the promise maker. When Abraham considered God's promise in the light of the integrity of his Lord, Abraham concluded that the miracle is a "slam dunk! (Of course he probably did not use those words!)

The writer to the Hebrews admonished the church to, ". . . **hold fast the profession of your faith without wavering; (for he is faithful that promised.)"** And though the church entered the picture many years later, Abraham knew the Spirit and the Integrity of the Faithfulness of The Faithful God! What Abraham very literally had faith in was—**God's faithfulness!** God was not an entity that had *at times* been faithful! Abraham did not know God to ever be less than faithful! Plus, God's faithfulness had always been more than satisfactory! El Shadai, literally translated, "The Almighty" and "The All Sufficient God, merited Abraham's trust but that was because God was faithful! And His faithfulness is what Abraham learned to trust in, honor and love.

A Feather from the Eagle's Wings

"When it seems that He is not answering your prayers, God's Sovereign Will is being done—NOT HIS NEGLECT!

CHAPTER 23

———◄•►———

FAITH'S LITMUS TEST

And being fully persuaded that, what he had promised, he was able also to perform. (Rom. 4:21)

God will not be a party to and neither will he endorse those things that are fakes, caricatures and misrepresentations of the authentic. A full persuasion is vital to receiving anything from God. Faith cannot coexist with anything thing that is less than faith! As soon as faith is mixed with anything true faith no longer exists! A question that I have been known to ask in order to make a point similar to this one is: "how many marbles can you put into an empty hole? The answers I usually get are

- as many as you can fit into the hole.
- Depends on the size of the hole
- Depend on the size of the marble

But these answers may work if I ask "How many marbles can you fit into a hole. But that is not the question! The question is, "How many marbles can you fit into an ***empty*** hole! The answer is *only one* because then you don't have an empty hole anymore! It has ceased to exist because the one marble is there.

Well, in order to have true and pure faith—nothing can be mixed with it! For as soon as you mix an alloy with it—you don't have true and pure faith anymore! If faith is blended to suspicion and doubt—God will have none of it! Be aware that faith must not rest **alone** in the fact that God promised—*faith must include the aspects of Divine Ability, Divine Knowledge, the Integrity of the Divine One, Divine Power and the Will of the Divine One!*

For, when faith's "litmus test" is given, those who are wise understand that *the measure of a person's expectation* for prayers answered is the defining dynamic—**not the strength and intensity of the desire!** When you consider the prospect of your prayer being answered—what do you truly expect will be the result of your petition? If **at the thought** of the great need that gave birth to your prayer, your stomach knots up and you break out in an anxiety attack—you have just defined your faith! If you find yourself looking for a plan "B"—you have just defined your faith! If you simply resign yourself to living without the prayer being answered—you have just defined *your faith!*

On the contrary, if at the thought of the thing "hoped for" you break out in a glad smile of anticipation and if you begin to rejoice at the mention of the expectation—you have defined your faith as something wonderful that is certain to happen! If you suddenly burst into praise or a song that praises God when the thought of your prayer being answered crosses your mind—you are a true "faither!"

CHAPTER 24

WHAT'S MISSING? "GREATER WORKS!"

No one can have faith in God to any greater degree than the measure of their intimate knowledge of Him! We have potentials *in* Him and *through* Him only as we *Know* Him! Our knowledge of Him gives birth to our expectations of Him. As we *Know* him we form understandings of Divine knowledge, Possibilities, Probabilities and Certainties of Him! As knowledge of God grows in one, there will be a progression from Divine Possibilities to Divine Probabilities and from there, ultimately, to the highest plateau of them all—***Divine Certainties!*** Wonder what Abraham's life would have been if he had lived after Jesus spoke those immortal Words, **"Verily, verily, I say unto you, He that believeth on me, the works that I do shall he do also; and greater works than these shall he do; because I go to my Father." (John 14:12)** At the time that He spoke these words, Jesus knew that it would not be long before He left his disciples to go through the greatest trauma of His life and of any life in the history of the world!

Jesus also knew what strength, power and comfort He was to His inner circle of disciples in this life. For, when they were lonely they had but to get close to Jesus! When they were in confusion and had questions in their hearts they came to Jesus Who doesn't merely have answers **He is the Ultimate Answer!** When they were sick or had sick loved ones—Jesus was their Healer! When they were sad and despondent—they got next to Jesus! He knew that He was their Everything! But also knew that soon He must go away or the Comforter could not come! (See John 16:7) So, at that time it was of paramount importance to the Son of God that His disciples **KNOW** that *when the Comforter comes they will have power in them <u>that they never had before!</u>* But right now please contemplate one of the greatest promises God ever made to man, **"I go to prepare a place for you. And if I go and prepare a place for you, I will come again, and receive you unto myself; that where I am, there ye may be also." (John 14:2b-3)**

By all means, Saints of God, let us slow way down in our thinking and ponder this issue! **Let's take it by the numbers! Jesus asserted:**

1. **"I go to prepare a place for you ... !"**
2. **"... I will come again ... !"**
3. **I will receive you unto myself!**
4. (Be careful here!) **... that where I am, there ye may be also!"**

Probably none of us will have a problem wrapping our head around statements 1-3. We all know He went to the Cross to prepare a place for us! But most people think that He was talking about preparing a place for us in Heaven.

Then, we all know that He always planned to come back!! Ultimately, we expected Him to receive us into His fold as His sheep and His children so we never had a problem believing those aspects of His promise.

But please pay strict attention to the last part of the promise! **"That where I <u>am</u> there ye <u>may be</u> also!"** Where was He? Where were they? Jesus said, **"That where I <u>am</u> . . ."**—present tense! Then He said, **". . . there ye <u>may</u> be also."** It would not have been surprising to hear that one of the disciples replied to him, "What do you mean? *We are* right here *where you are* right now. Geographically speaking, ***<u>Jesus was with His disciples</u> sitting at the table at "Last Supper!"*** So where was He **that they were not?** The answer, Dear Reader is ***He was in the position of <u>The Sonship!</u>*** Though Jesus had elevated the disciples from the status of servants and now called them friends,(John 15:15) it was always the supreme plan of the Father that we be brothers to His Son, Jesus and to one another! (See Heb. 2:11-12 & Rom. 8:29) But For us to become Jesus' brothers we had to become ***the Father's sons!***

Now let us take stock of ***the Power and Potential of that Promise*** that was mentioned at the beginning of this chapter; the promise of our entering into the sonship with Jesus! Without considering the quality of His miracles let us just take into consideration the ***number*** of the miracles that Jesus wrought. **John 21:25 "And there are also many other things which Jesus did, the which, if they should be written every one, I suppose that even the world itself could not contain the books that should be written."** Jesus worked so many miracles that the Apostle, John supposed that even the world itself could not contain the books that should be written to record those deeds. If we will ponder that reality and add to it the fact that Jesus promised, "... **greater than these shall ye do ...,**" **(John 14:12)** we will get a glimpse of the magnitude of the power, authority and privilege the Church has today and how far beneath our rights and liberties we are living! Nevertheless, because many in the Church don't *Know* these truths—the Church remains in a rut and continues to run on a treadmill of man's busyness!

Many churches are entered into an undeclared competition of building larger and grander monuments to man as they define success in terms of the numbers that occupy the sanctuary, how many are in their choir, how large and opulent their building is and how much "fun" they have at their church! The success of the Church used to be measured by how many souls were actually saved, how many had been healed and delivered from demonic influence and the like! But in those days the Church knew God differently than most of the Church does today!

The question begs to be asked and answered, "Where are the greater works than Jesus did? Certainly the numbers in our Churches outnumber those in the following of Jesus! He was just one man! We out number Him millions to one! Yet we have not the number or the quality of miracles that He had on a daily basis! Could it be because of WHAT WE DON'T _KNOW_?

A Feather from the Eagle's Wings

Whatever will attract the flesh will distract the spirit!

CHAPTER 25

A "GAME" GOD PLAYS

Heb 6:16For men verily by the greater: and an oath for confirmation *is* to them an end of all strife.

I want to discuss the notion of *God promising man*—just as a point of information; just so **you will know why God plays the "like man" game; "the promise game!"**!

When man makes a commitment or predicts what He is going to do in the future, he causes others to have an expectation. We call those intents—*"promises."* We think of a promise as something that has to occur sometimes over time and often by a process—but definitely in the future. When finite man makes the promise, because the future event is dependent upon man to accomplish the thing—we call that intent a "promise;" a promise that is oft times more tenuous than it is certain to come to fruition. A promise is very much like insurance. Insurance is no more reliable *than the character of the insurer* is dependable. Never forget that the promise is no surer to be fulfilled than the integrity of the promise maker.

So that you will **Know** that there is often a lack of certainty in man's promise, please note this illustration. It is a fact that a verbal promise to give something that is not owed is not enforceable in a court of law! If someone promises to give you fifty thousand dollars and they don't give it—you cannot sue and have a judge enforce the promise! It was only what we call an "empty promise! The "promise" is not an enforceable contract because for a contract to be enforceable there must something called, "consideration." That simply means that all parties whose signatures are on the contract must get something out of the deal. In the case of a promise that does not enrich all of the signees somehow—that promise is non-enforceable! This renders the promise nothing more than empty words! I guess a good analogy would be the question, "What do you call a leader that no one is following? Answer: "a man taking a walk!" A promise that is made by a person who cannot or will not keep his word is simply a statement of fantasy!

Heb 6:16For men verily swear by the greater: and an oath for confirmation *is* to them an end of all strife.

Heb 6:17Wherein God, willing more abundantly to shew unto the heirs of promise the immutability of his counsel, confirmed *it* by an oath:

God is so concerned that His children accept His Word as Truth that He is "... **willing more abundantly to shew unto the heirs of promise the immutability of his counsel** ...!" That He cares with an abundance of concern causes Him to play *"the man game."*

To reiterate, in recognition and sensitivity toward man's frailties, God often defers His Power and All *Knowing* and "plays" with man according to man's weaknesses. For example, when God wanted man to know with copious and absolute certainty that God meant what He said, God used a ploy that men use with one another to allay and calm their fears and apprehension concerning another's integrity. The method He used to confirmed His Word of Promise to man was—to swear; to "... **confirmed** *it* (His promise) by an oath ... !**" For, when **men ... swear by the greater**" (something dearer and of greater value than themselves) they intend for the oath to be confirmation and verification of the truthfulness of their promise. They may say, for instance "I swear on my mother's grave!" Or, "I swear on a stack of Bibles!" Those words, for many people, *seal the deal!*

Feathers from the Eagle's Wings

*"When you know that you are spiritually weak—**Don't Make Any Major Decisions!**"*

CHAPTER 26

———⇒◦⇐———

PERFECT IMPERFECTION?

(Num 23:19) **God is not a man, that he should lie; neither the son of man, that he should repent: hath he said, and shall he not do it? or hath he spoken, and shall he not make it good?**

Every good gift and every perfect gift is from above, and cometh down from the Father of lights, <u>with whom is no variableness, neither shadow of turning.</u> (Jas 1:17)

- God, of course, makes certain that mankind *Knows* that God "**. . . is not a man . . .!**" In light of this truth, it naturally follows that *<u>God cannot tell a lie!</u>*" Further reasoning, "**. . . neither . . .**" is He "**. . . the son of man that he should repent . . . !** Men lie because they repent (change their minds).

- God does not lie and He cannot change His mind. That is why He never rescinds or backs out on His Promise! For as James said, **"God . . . with whom** is no variableness . . . !" (James 1:17) When, in scripture, God *"repented"* this *in no way* meant that He changed His mind! Don't forget—*in Him* there is not even the **"shadow of turning!"** (Jas. 1:17) We Know that He declared "**. . . the end from the beginning, and from ancient times the things that are not yet done, saying, My counsel shall stand, and I will do all my pleasure.** (Isa 46:10)

- So "changing His Mind was not a spur of the moment decision or a whim of thought—He always knew what He was going to do!

Here we are again speaking of the Immutability of God! Understand this, Dear One, the only way for God to change would be to improve His self or degrade and cheapen Himself by diminishing Himself. This He cannot do! He cannot improve Himself because there is no standard to which He is inferior; there is no standard higher than the perfectness of His perfection! And He is too perfect to become imperfect! You see, He and only He would have to announce His Own imperfections because there is no being so perfect as to note in Him any flaw or defect. Additionally, **if He rendered Himself <u>imperfect</u>** He would do it to such a quality of perfection that He would **only be <u>"Perfectly Imperfect!"</u>**

Feathers From the Eagle's Wings

You engage in futility who endeavor to free the body while the mind is bound.

CHAPTER 27

———❖◀❖———

GOD PROMISED?

This Chapter's Key to Understanding the Surety of God's Promise

". . . there is never the slightest chance that the Promises of God may fail because the Promise is inexorably linked to Divine Integrity, Will and Power!

Everything God says is a decree and when God decrees a thing it can no more fail to come about *than God can come to death!* It should be completely preposterous and absurd to everyone who confesses to be a Believer in God that God would have to promise anything! **"But, God Promised!"** Why should it be said that God Who places a law into existence every time he utters a Word—promises! He is unchanging because He is Unchangeable! He is Unchangeable so His Words are Unchangeable! His Words are Immutable because God Himself is Immutable! His counsel cannot mutate or be mutated by any power, condition or desire apart from Him!

Every student of God and the Word of God must understand that our God doesn't want his children to merely memorize His Word—He has determined that they will **Know** some of his reasoning for some of His decisions. Therefore, He explains why He swore that he would keep His Promises and why His Children can have confidence in those Promises. Note the following passages from the Book of Hebrews.

"For men verily swear by the greater: and an oath for confirmation is to them an end of all strife." "Wherein God, willing more abundantly to shew unto the heirs of promise the immutability of his counsel, confirmed it by an oath . . . ." (Heb 6:16-17) KJV

This is just one more time that God plays the "man game." The "man game" is when God Powers down and reduces His methods to a level that man can easily relate to. Men have the tendency to place value on everything they own or appreciate. That value will be more or less depending on the importance that it has in their heart. Often, the thing is valued so much that it acquires a worth that deems it almost sacred. Men consign to some things a preciousness that is greater even than their own life. So, that most precious and highly prized treasure is the object that they swear by. **"For when God made promise to Abraham, <u>because he could swear by no greater, he sware by himself</u> . . . ." Heb 6:13 KJV**

For noble men of honor and integrity, *an honorable man swearing by uttering an oath seals everything!* Now, God could have simply announced His Will (His Counsel) and required that man understand It, surrender to It and live according to It. However, God pronounced His Counsel and then, because He knows the significance that man places on an oath, He swore that His "Counsel would stand" (see Isa. 46:10) and that He would make good on His Promise! Ultimately, He ". . . **confirmed**" His counsel "**. . . by an oath.**"

"**That by two immutable things, in which it was impossible for God to lie, we might have a strong consolation, who have fled for refuge to lay hold upon the hope set before us . . . .**" (Heb. 6:18 KJV)

The ". . . **two immutable things, <u>in which it was impossible for God to lie</u> . . .**" are His Counsel and His Oath! His Counsel cannot be altered because as He is Eternal so are His Judgments! Remembering that God declared ". . . **the end from the beginning, and from ancient times the things that are not yet done . . . ," (Isa 46:10 KJV)** the true believer can readily understand and rejoice in celebration that the Oath and Promise of God cannot fail or be frustrated! In His Omniscience and His Omnipresence, the Eternal God Knows all and Has All Power to fulfill His Promise, saying in Jer. 1:12, "**. . . I will hasten my word to perform it.**"

Again, I say, "**Everything God says is a decree and when God decrees a thing it can no more fail to come about *than God can come to death!*" The challenge for every believer who desires to see the Promises of God come to fruition is to wait patiently for the fullness of the time to occur. This time is to make believers know beyond any shadow of doubt whether they have patience to endure to the end. There is always an period of time that only the Sovereign Will of God can determine, between the promise and its fulfillment. The True Believer must hear in the deepest echelons of his spirit man the promise of God found in Hab. 2:3 KJV **"For the vision is yet for an appointed time, but at the end it shall speak, and not lie: though it tarry, wait for it; because it will surely come, it will not tarry."**

Remember, Precious Heart, God only calls His statements of future happenings and divine intent, "Promises" because of man's view toward those things that were pledged prior to their fulfillment. The true believer **knows** that when God says a thing is going to take place He speaks a divine edict! He declares a law! When God says what will take place—*in the Heart and Mind of God it is done at the moment He declares it* although time may have to take its toll before the Utterance is manifested to man! The person of faith doesn't place the greatest emphasis on the *when* or *the timeline* of God's Promise but accentuates the *unconditional conclusive certainty* that the Promise will come to pass!

Man knows that man's promises may fail because the sureness of the promise is no greater than the integrity and the ability of the promise maker! However, there is never the slightest chance that the promises of God may fail because the promise is inexorably linked to Divine Integrity, Will and Power! As God is Lord over all, so is He Master over the future where His promises live! When the Saints of God know this we will have a faith in God that will never waver, never falter and never know defeat!

God promised! Is God's Promise a waste of words? No! God's Promises are God's means of the Infinite One interacting with His finite creatures. It is the Timeless God dealing with His Children who are restricted by and often at the mercy of time. God's Promises are God's Way of communicating to His Body those things that are indicators of His great and loving concern that He ever has for them.

Feathers from the Eagle's Wings

"Our Omnipresent God cannot go anywhere because
He's already there!"

CHAPTER 28

———◆◆◆———

LESS TRULY IS MORE!

A Key to Understanding the Purity and the Effectiveness of Faith

". . . it is not the size of the faith that works miracles!"

Abraham lived too early to hear the words of James 1:6-7. **But let him ask in faith, nothing wavering. For he that wavereth is like a wave of the sea driven with the wind and tossed. For let not that man think that he shall receive any thing of the Lord.** But Abraham probably knew the spirit of this truth!

In this passage, the Apostle James encourages the church to **"ask in faith—nothing wavering."** Jesus teaches in Luke 17:6, *". . . If ye had faith as a grain of mustard-seed . . ."* there would be no end to the miracles that you would produce in the name of the Lord. In other words, you don't have to have a mountain full or an ocean of faith! Just *". . . **faith as a grain of mustard seed . . . !"*** At this point in time it is necessary that we examine the mustard seed. The mustard is between 1 and 2 millimeters round which make it one of the world's smallest seeds. So, why would Jesus use the mustard seed as an example of the believer's faith?

Well, it is a very aromatic seed with a sharp, pungent odor and taste! All that it is suggests that it has properties that will affect its surroundings! The mustard seed is a most fitting example of the powers and promises of faith! First of all the size of the seed has nothing to do with its effectiveness! It is not the size of the seed that matters—it is the purity of the seed that matters! **Though small—it is one hundred percent mustard seed!** It has been said that *"it is not the size of the dog that is in the fight* that makes the difference—*it is the size of the fight that is in the dog* that determines the victor!" Similarly, it is not the size of the faith that works miracles!

> Rather, it is the purity of the faith that:
> makes laws that change long held traditions
> cures the incurable **h**olds bondage in bondage and
> **r**esurrects the dead!

But the issue of the size of the mustard seed doesn't end there! For the tiny mustard seed produces plants and flowers that are larger than the seeds! Plus, the seed reproduces itself many times on the plant! Talk about leveraging your potential!

"If ye had faith as a grain of mustard-seed . . . ." also brings to mind the fact that in addition to its distinctive size, the mustard seed has an unmistakable fragrance. Its odor is so sharp as to be virtually tangible. And (for its

size) no plant has had a greater effect on this world than the mustard seed!

Remember, Child of God, **faith is about *knowing*!** And *true knowing* (**true faith**) is about POWER; *power to effect* CHANGE in yourself and your world; *power to* CREATE the world of your dreams *in your world!* And *true knowing* provides *the power to* WIN battles that you have always lost!

Faith is so very like the mustard seed! Consider this: what if you should take a handful of mustard seed and divide them in two parts? One part you plant in fertile soil and the other part you save in a box and that you place on a closet shelf. The seeds that you water and nourish with plant food and provide the proper light for will grow and produce a plant that will bear more life giving seed.

The box of seed that you have saved on the closet shelf will still be there just as you left it! Count them! They are all there. You are not to be praised and applauded for your faithfulness in not losing a one of them! Rather, it is appalling, disgraceful and reprehensible that you have denied the seeds the freedom of reaching their potential!

Perhaps the greatest loss in Churches today is the loss of potential! Pulpits are empty because ministers refused to pay the price to reach their potential in becoming spiritually prepared ministers! Choirs are missing many of the best voices because singers got distracted and left the choir loft to sing on the secular stage! Sunday School classes are being taught mediocre and oft times un-anointed lessons because teachers refuse to study, fast and pray! Sickness and disease run rampant in many families of the church because generational curses have not been broken by faithful healers! If there is one thing that church folk do well it is—THEY DIE WELL! They die well because few people pay the cost of developing the kind of *knowing* that works miracles! And they die because they are surrounded by people in the Church and out of it who expect them to. There is an unquestionable and absolute lack of faith in many churches today.

Wait, Precious Hearts! Stop for a moment and consider the proposal of Jesus! What "*. . . If ye had faith as a grain of mustard-seed . . .*" when Satan comes to call? How would you change your world and the world around you? Imagine what could happen if the church did study God and His Word **not to merely know more** but **to become something more?** "See yourself walking through the grocery store being approached by a man in a battery operated "scooter." You pause to say "Hello" to him. Then you ask him if you might pray for him. With a look of mild surprise his simply nods his head in agreement. At His consent you gently place your hand on his legs, whisper a few words and then you see a look of wondrous surprise envelop his face as he begins to slowly move his legs! He moves them a little faster and then the realization floods his heart! He knows that it is true! He can move his legs! All of a sudden with a shout of joy he leaps from the scooter and dances a jig around you! Finally, with tears rolling down his face and a smile that seems to be as big as the Texas sky, He comes face to face with you and wonders, "How did you do you do that? With both of his hands in both of yours you begin to teach him Jesus and His great love!

What marvelous acts you would do if you determined to *know* God intimately; *Know* Him as He longs to reveal Himself to man? What Glory would be His because *in His Name*—you acted! What miracles would confirm your faith and your doctrine—all because you came to **know** God!

A Feather From the Eagle's Wings

God doesn't need or want your advice!

CHAPTER 29

PERFECT LOVE INSPIRES RADICAL LOVE

A Key to understanding the Power of Love is found in this Chapter

"One of the elemental strengths of love is radical courage!"

When Jesus was seen by a boat load of very frightened disciples on a dark and stormy night, this sighting was in all probability an answer to Peter's prayer. Picture it! The waves were so high that the ship was in danger of being swamped; at risk of being turned over! The winds were blowing so hard and the sea was so rough that the winds and the waves presented to the disciples a certainty of death by drowning. Now add to that scenario the great love that Peter had for His Master. Jesus had been for hours separated from His disciples and when a loved one is missing, the time apart may seem to be multiplied—possibly a hundred fold!

Jesus was both the Love of Peter's life and his Divine Security Blanket. Jesus was Peter's Comfort and his Comforter; his Protector and his Protection; his Answer and his Solution! Note that when Peter's mother-in—law was sick having a fever, Peter simply depended on Jesus to handle the problem. (Matt 8:14-15) And when Jesus and Peter had taxes to pay and didn't have the money to pay them, Jesus just told Peter to, "... **go thou to the sea, and cast a hook, and take up the fish that first cometh up. And when thou hast opened his mouth, thou shalt find a piece of money: that take, and give unto them for me and thee.**" (Matt 17:27) KJV

So, when Peter was in great fear for his safety during the storm his great love for Jesus, coupled with his dependence on his Lord resulted in Peter walking on the water to go to Jesus. (See Matt. 14:29)

I have often said that *"I'd rather be walking on the water with Jesus than be in the boat with other folk!"* For, there, on the water with Jesus, I **Know** that I am in the presence of the Love of my life and the Master of all the world and there is no safer place on earth.

Is there any power as strong as love? As fearful as Peter was for his life while he was in the safety of the boat, how much more precarious would logic and reason suggest his situation would be *when he got out of the boat?* The ship was the only safety that he had and yet he was willing to step out on the very waters that threatened his life when he was in the security of the boat! But all who know the influence that love has on the one who is loved knows that *one of the elemental strengths of love is radical courage!*

The axiom and adage is very true, "*Necessity is the mother of invention.*" In this case Peter's love for His Master caused "*necessity*" to birth in Peter the absolutely radical notion of him getting to Jesus *by any means necessary*. Even in these days it has been declared by one soul, "Ain't no mountain high enough; ain't no valley low enough; ain't no river wide enough to keep me away from you, Babe!" Peter couldn't wait for his Love to come to him! He had to get to Jesus! ". . . **Perfect love** . . . truly . . . **casteth out fear** . . ." (1Jn 4:18)

Isn't it remarkable that Peter did not ask to "**walk on the water <u>with</u> Jesus**" but "**bid me come <u>unto thee</u> on the water.**" (Matt. 14:28) Peter was not asking for a miracle. He was not trying to make a name for himself—he was asking to go to the One he loved best in the world! But, how did he expect to get there? However Peter was to get to Jesus in that storm of rain and wind; the storm that was so wild with waves that threatened to overturn the boat—**it was going to take a miracle!** Of course, walking on the stormy sea would be one way but Peter knew that he was talking to Jesus, the one Who invented the proverbial, "BOX!" Jesus could have as easily told Peter to swim to Him in the stormy sea or He could have made Peter fly to him! Peter did not care **as long as he just got to Jesus!** So Peter's cry and plea to his Lord was, "**bid me come <u>unto thee</u> on the water.**"

True love will make the lover think out of the box! The disciples were not able to control the boat and row to Jesus because ". . . **the ship was now in the midst of the sea, tossed with waves: for the wind was contrary.**" (Mat

14:24) But Peter was determined that nothing was going to separate him from His Lord and his Friend that night!

What if the entire Church of the Living God would come to love our Savior so much that we said, as did Paul in Rom. 8:38-39, **"For I am persuaded that neither death, nor life, nor angels, nor principalities, nor powers, nor things present,**

Nor things to come, nor height, nor depth, nor any other creature, shall be able to separate us from the love of God, which is in Christ Jesus our Lord."

Peter was not looking at any renown and praise that his feat would bring to him. He saw only that he had to get to Jesus! If he considered it at all, the fact that it would take a miracle was secondary to the loving heart of Peter! Hence, the storm was incidental to the true essence of this episode in the lives of the Christ and Peter! The storm simply provided a backdrop wherein a drama that was filled with fear, jeopardy and the daring of faith and love could unfold!

The developing student who is reading this exposition must now consider some very strange developments in this passage of scripture! Consider Matt. 14:24 where the Apostle, Matthew, very clearly observes that "... **the wind was contrary.**

Clearly, Peter knew that the wind was contrary, else why had he been afraid? He had seen the climatic conditions and was very much aware of the storm. What happened to him when he perceived that it was his Greatest Love out there walking on the water? His fear of the storm could not compete with the opportunity to be reunited with his Jesus and the storm then became inconsequential to him! He Who was His Savior; his Lord and his Friend was nearby and that became Peter's entire focus! And when Jesus uttered just the one word, "Come!" natural law was rescinded and a new order of the day was initiated! That the water was not solid—did not matter one whit! That Peter was truly in uncharted territory was of no significance! His Jesus gave him permission to transcend the laws of liquid matter and break the law of gravity and go where no mere man had gone before! The love that Peter had for Jesus was so powerful that it completely overcame his very real fear of the deadly storm. So, Peter ". . . **walked on the water to go to Jesus.**" (Matt. 14:29) He literally walked on the water or perhaps he was walking on the strength of his faith as he was driven by his radical love for the Love of God!

A Feather From the Eagle's Wings

*Never ask people to pray for you based on their relationship to You—ask them to pray for you based on **what you believe their relationship is to God!***

CHAPTER 30

———⟫•◦•⟪———

THE FIVE LOOKS

A Key to the amazing truth that, "What you see will determine what you do!"

*"Look at Matt 14:30, "**But when he saw** the wind boisterous, he was afraid; and beginning to sink, he cried, saying, Lord, save me."*

What you are determines what you will think. What you think determines what you will see and what you see will determine what you do! There were five times that Peter looked and saw things that were influences that each succeeding scene in this fateful episode in his life hinged on that night! These bear looking at!

The "**First Look**" and the first scene that Peter and the disciples saw was the storm tossing the boat on the sea. How do you see the primordial elemental forces of nature at their worse without also coming face to face with your own weakness and vulnerability? How do you witness firsthand the awesome and unlimited power of God without acknowledging your own frailty and defenselessness? When there is a power that is so great and uncaring for your wellbeing as to hold your stronghold and your security in disdain and contempt—how do you maintain any modicum of self respect and self control? When you know that the boat you are in is the only thing that can succor and support you and the storm is tossing that "safety net" around as if it were nothing at all—what do you do and what are your options? Such was the plight of Peter and the rest of the disciples who quickly learned that they could not navigate on those waters.

Then Peter looked the second time and saw an ethereal, ghostly figure walking on the water! Peter knew not that It was Jesus walking on those dashing waves! He thought it was a spirit, a ghost or a phantom! Now they are in double trouble! First they had the thrashing, foaming sea and the blasting winds and blinding rain to deal with! Now they believe they have to face demons and possibly the "undead!" How do they survive this new threat! How do they fight a specter from the grave? These grown men were in such a state of fear that they cried out, **"It is a spirit!"**

We can only imagine the sudden thrill that coursed through Peter when he heard the voice of Jesus above the wind and the waves! Jesus said, as only the Prince of Peace can utter, **"Be of good cheer; it is I; be not afraid." KJV** (Matt. 14:27) What a wonderful encouragement these words were to Peter! What exquisite promise underscored these words of comfort, promise and spiritual insight! For, what Jesus was very literally saying is, *"No matter how horrific your situation is or how deplorable and hopeless you* *believe your plight—**you have no reason to be discomfited in any way;*** you have no ***cause to fear because—I am here!*** *And <u>where I am</u>, <u>Heaven is</u> and <u>all of the powers and resources of God are brought to bear!</u>"* Note that He didn't say, "Don't be sad!" Neither is He merely saying, "Wipe your eyes!" Jesus is saying so much more than "Don't worry!" Rather, Jesus ordered the disciples to step into a very positive glad place! He ordered them and expected them to obey His Will as if what He said was just the most natural thing for frightened men to do. He said, **"Be of good cheer!"**

When Peter heard these words, he acted in a most peculiar manner. At the first, he thought he was looking at a phantom or a spirit and it is very unlikely that he would ask a fearsome ghost to allow him to approach him! Why would Peter ask to go the very thing that had caused him such dread; such trepidation? Ah, but let us not forget that the Prince of Peace had just spoken and commanded the disciples to **"be not afraid."**

Now experience **the "Third Look!"** This look was focused by Jesus. His Peace was an all-prevailing calm! At His Word, His Serenity and Tranquility permeated and saturated the mind and heart of Peter when Jesus announced His identity and His Presence. He then commanded Peter to not fear! This command worked on two fronts:

1. it dismissed the spirit of fear and anxiety and quelled the anticipation of catastrophe and
2. *it gave a new focus and a new purpose to Peter through a new **Knowing** !*

Then Peter did the unthinkable! He asked to go to Jesus! Jesus did not have a small canoe or a kayak to offer Peter! But He is the King of Kings and **"Where the word of a king *is, there is* power. (**Ecc. 8:4) And He did have His Word! So Jesus simply and profoundly said, **"Come!"** Instantly, Peter took just one look at his heart's desire and the mounting waves were only distant memories! When *The Knowing* took over, the lion-like roar of the sea was no more than the purring of a kitten! Despite the boisterous winds, no longer was Peter driven and restricted by the paralyzing, debilitating terror that had his mind and heart in a death grip! Peace flooded his soul! His Peace; the Peace of His Lord brought such a calm to Peter that getting out of the dubious safety of the boat was as natural for him to do as putting on his sandals.

"And when Peter was come down out of the ship, <u>he walked on the water</u>, to go to Jesus." (Matt. 14:29) In all probability, Peter's thoughts as he walked on the water were not on the improbability of his act. In all likelihood, he gave no thought to the uniqueness of his situation. His mind and his heart were solely on the Love of God! He only had eyes for Jesus! And as long as he allowed for no distractions—he walked on the water! As long as Earth's reality was left to the earthly—*he did the heavenly!* He transcended the laws of Earth! He did the miraculous! **". . . He walked on the water, to go to Jesus."**

Now look at Matt 14:30 and witness **the "Fourth Look!"** **"But when he saw the wind boisterous, he was afraid . . . ."** For just a moment, Peter had a lapse in his attention and began to be afraid as Earth's reality eclipsed his heart-felt devotion to his Lord. It was then that Peter's emphasis and devotion changed from his Love to his self! Oh, how like Peter the Children of God can be. *When it suits us—we can focus on Jesus and for a time do the godlike thing. But, in a moment of indecision, fear, lust or greed, we take our eyes off Jesus. And in that instant—Satan capitalizes and takes advantage of the moment!* ***And we begin to sink!***

". . . and beginning to sink, he cried, saying, Lord, save me." This is the fifth look! And what a look it was! Peter began to sink after losing his focus and fixating on the natural surroundings! True to form, the natural fought hard against the spiritual! However, this time the natural won over the spiritual! Despite his having overcome natural laws; despite the victory over his fears; despite the miracle of walking on the water—**Peter began to sink!** Now, he knows that he has done the extraordinary! Now, he finally sees that he has accomplished the miraculous but ***now <u>he</u> needs a miracle!***

Saints, don't wait for the untoward to occur before you appreciate and celebrate the Favor, Mercy and Grace of God! Take time to savor every moment you spend in the presence of the Divine. Don't let one moment of your time with the Power of powers slip away unnoticed, uncelebrated and unloved! As you love our Lord—love every moment spent in His Presence!

". . . Lord, save me!"

Yes! Peter began to sink! But not to worry! The Miracle Worker is on the scene! I just wish that I could see this "Fifth Look" from Peter's vantage point! From the depths of the sea that is threatening to swallow him up whole,

Peter looks up into the eyes of his Savior **"... saying, Lord, save me!"**

What do you see, Peter? What do the eyes of the Savior look like when He is so proud of the steps that you have taken into the unknown; steps into territory that is for you, uncharted? Then what do His eyes reveal when He is so ashamed that you dismissed Him so quickly simply because you chose to see Earth's nightmare rather than Heaven's Dream? How does your Jesus, in one breath, know His pride in the moment of the great accomplishment that you made by reason of your faith in Him and then, in the next breath, know that you now live in the moment that you decided to *no longer walk as a son of God?* He knows that you chose to act in the cowardice of those whose hearts and mind are only of this earth! What is the look of disappointment that fills His countenance when He sees you, Peter, stop walking on the water and start to sink? Then, the sight of you sinking forces to Him to wrench His Mind from the joyous elation that was His moments ago when He witnessed His protégé do the miraculous! What are His embarrassment and His vexation as He realizes that His hope for Apostleship is still able to forget that he is "Peter, the Rock" and once again become merely "Simon" of his parent's birth? It is clear to the Lord of Lords that until now *only a God has walked on water* **but you, Peter, just did that god-like thing!** Now, Peter, how can Jesus ignore the stark contrast; the unmistakable dissimilarity and the negative comparison to your amazing feat? Now He has to see the ugly, mean and dark moment when you allowed other things and other realities to eclipse this splendid moment in which you truly walked as the son of a God? Now, the moment when you walked as His son no longer has any life or merit **because you chose to allow the earthily to eclipse the Heavenly.** You have chosen to replace the Living Vision with the temporal view. You, Peter, *walked as a son of the Son of God* but <u>*now you walk as do the children of a lesser god!*</u>

"And immediately Jesus stretched forth his hand, and caught him, and said unto him, O thou of little faith, wherefore didst thou doubt?" (Matt 14:31) KJV

Yes, Peter, you *Know* your Jesus as one Who can enable you to walk on the water in a great storm! And you *Know* him as the One Whom you can call on in the moment of your failure! But you also *Know* Him as the One Who will never confuse your failure with your value! You called on Him and He heard you! He heard you and immediately came to your aid! He used all that He was to save you! With His Eyes He saw you going down into what the devil intended to be your watery grave. With His ears He heard your plaintive cry for help. With His Loving Arms that are truly extensions of His Loving Heart, He reached out to you! Bracing Himself on His strong legs and using His back muscles He lifted you. He lifted you because the Love and Compassion that filled His great Heart with concern for you, Peter, would not allow Him to do less! He is, after all the Loving Savior!

"…and said unto him, O thou of little faith, wherefore didst thou doubt?" (Matt 14:31 KJV)

Oh, He rebuked you! But He also gave you a life lesson as to the reason that He knows that you are of **"little faith"—you doubted!** He did not accuse you of having no faith at all because He knows that you did walk on the water! But that was as close as He came to acknowledging that you did the miraculous! He said little about the miracle but you did **"walk on the water to go to Jesus!"** Note: Matt 14:29 KJV, **"And when Peter was come down out of the ship, he walked on the water, <u>to go to Jesus."</u>**

Jesus voiced His disappointment at the fact, Peter, that your faith lacked stamina—*but He saved you!* He never mentioned to you that He was proud of you for walking on the water but HE LIFTED YOU UP OUT OF THE HUNGRY JAWS OF DEATH and **HE SAVED YOU!**

He reached the strong arm of His Love out to you in the briny deep, in the midst of a tempest and **HE SAVED YOU!** And you knew that He was seeing you through eyes that had never lost their love and compassion. As a matter of fact, you knew that your Jesus was born for such a time as this; the time of your greatest shame and self condemnation from your birth until this moment!

If ever this writer begins to sink, he prays that the first eyes he looks into will be those of his loving and caring Savior, Jesus Christ!

A Feather From the Eagle's Wings

Whenever you stop walking on the water <u>you will begin to sink!</u>

CHAPTER 31

THE THREE-FOLD PLAN

A Key to realizing the reason that Peter walked on the water with Jesus!

"God intended for Peter to experience this miracle!"

The reader must know that the All Knowing of our God **Who declared "... the end from the beginning, and from ancient times *the things* that are not *yet* done (Isa 46:10)** was fully aware of all that was going to take place on the fateful night that Peter walked on the water. You must realize that when Jesus and Peter walked on the water they did so because from the foundation of the world, *God intended for Peter to experience this miracle!*

The Plan of God was at least three-fold.

1. He wanted Peter to experience His Power!
2. He wanted to Peter to come face to face with his own weakness and vulnerability!

3. He wanted Peter to be absolutely clear in his *Knowing* that Jesus will be the Ever Present, Savior!

Mat 14:31 **"And immediately Jesus stretched forth *his* hand, and caught him, and said unto him, O thou of little faith, wherefore didst thou doubt?"**

Though the astute student may sometimes hear the rebuke in the voice of Jesus, the truly spiritually astute will hear something else also. Note Jesus' acknowledgement of Peter's faith. "Peter," Jesus remarked, "You are not devoid of all faith! You do have **"little faith!"** Please, Precious Hearts don't miss the true message here! Don't let the power of *"little faith"* pass you by! The disciple, Peter, actually did walk on the water **to go to Jesus!** We know that He got there because when he began to sink ". . . <u>**immediately Jesus stretched forth *his* hand, and caught him.**</u>" Usually, when folk talk about this episode in Peter's life much is said about the fact that he saw the winds boisterous and began to sink when he took his eyes off Jesus and these things should be mentioned! But, we need to celebrate Peter's miracle also! **He actually walked on the water!** *When is the last time you did it?*

I guess this is as good a time as any to make sure you understand that *a miracle is not determined by the thing that happened* **but by the circumstances that prevailed when the phenomenon occurred**. Because, to tell the truth I have walked on water! Of course, the water was frozen when I walked on it! My miracle was that I didn't slip on the ice and break my head!

Next, I would most assuredly be remiss in my responsibility to tell the whole truth if I failed to address Jesus' admonition of Peter, **"O thou of little faith, wherefore didst thou doubt?"** Faith is not really measured in amounts *but in purity.* Faith must be mixed with nothing! It must remain undiluted. Nothing can dilute faith but that which comes from natural logic and earthly reasoning. And understand this clearly—faith is not anti logic! **It is just superior to logic!**

Peter was rebuked because in a moment of weakness he completely forgot that he walked *and could still walk on water if he would only believe!* For, Jesus never did recall or rescind His permission for Peter to "... **come** ..." and walk on the water! Peter's failure was not only in his sinking but in his *not getting back up by the strength of his faith!* Though it is to Peter's credit that he remembered the strong Arm of Jesus and cried out for help—Jesus was ashamed of Peter because he should have simply stood back up and continued to walk on the strength of his faith! Many who know me, the author of this book, know that I have been a horseman for many years. There is an old adage among some Western horse-folk that says, "There ain't a horse that cain't be rode and there ain't a cowboy that cain't be throwed!" Failure is a part of the human existence. Errors in judgments are made! People don't always hit the target they aim for! Sometimes we have lapses in our attention span! Yes, we do get distracted! But we need always to get back in the saddle again after we fall off the horse! We need to try again after we fail to succeed! We must learn to refocus our attention if we get distracted! But, whatever we do WE MUST NOT QUIT! WE CAN SUCCEED THE NEXT TIME OR THE NEXT TIME OR THE

NEXT TIME etc. You get the drift! As I have taught for many years, "Most people don't fail because they don't try hard! They fail because *they don't try hard long enough!*"

Because Jesus never retracted His spoken authority that enabled Peter to walk on the water, the Word, **"Come"** which Jesus said to Peter was still in effect! It still had the Power to work the miracle! So, Peter, "... **wherefore didst thou doubt?"** Why did you *continue* to doubt? Why didn't you know that what the Master did once—He can still do? Why did you not have faith in what He had done **to the extent that it became a *Knowing* in you <u>that He would do it again?</u>** God is a God of the *"Divine Precedence!"* He is, "**Jesus Christ the same yesterday, and today, and forever."** (Heb 13:8) What He has done—He will do! What He has said, He is yet saying! **For I *am* the LORD, I change not.** (Mal 3:6) Once God uses you; once He works through you, you are endowed with that anointing and that power and are authorized to continue to do that miracle unless God rescinds the authorization! **"For, the gifts and calling of God *are* without repentance."** (Rom 11:29) Jesus may not have been as put out by Peter sinking as He was by Peter staying sunken! Do you recall when Jesus, Himself, sank under the heavy weight of the Cross of Crucifixion? And do you remember that the same Jesus Who said in John 18:37, **"To this end was I born, and for this cause came I into the world . . . ,"** "prayed, saying, **O my Father, if it be possible, let this cup pass from me: nevertheless not as I will, but as thou wilt."** (Matt 26:39 KJV) So, you see, Jesus was well accustomed to the concept of "sinking." What bothered Jesus was the fact that He would not enjoy an experience with Peter that was similar to that which He enjoyed with Adam in the

Garden of Eden when the Voice of the Lord walked with Adam in the cool of the day. (See Gen. 3:8) Imagine, Dear Child of the King, what may have occurred if Peter had just calmed himself down and taken stock of the fact that he had actually walked on the water! What if he had just had *The Knowing* that what Jesus did once—He could do again and instead of asking Jesus to give him a "hand up" he had asked for permission to climb back up on the water to renew his walk with Son of God! What would Jesus have talked to him about after He showed Jesus such phenomenal faith? Would Peter have come away from the experience rejoicing in grateful amazement as did the men who talked with Jesus on the road to Emmaus in Luke 24:13-32?

Herein is a fitting example for all who have been known to fall. We are admonished in the Word of God to not give up when we fall or when we fail. **"My little children, these things write I unto you, that ye sin not. And if any man sin, we have an advocate with the Father, Jesus Christ the righteous . . . . (1 John 2:1 KJV)** The only thing that is worse than falling or sinking is staying down; staying sunken! Get up, Saints! Build yourself up on your most Holy Faith! (See Jude 20)

CHAPTER 32

———◆◆◆———

DOUBT, THE HEART PROBLEM—FAITH, THE HEART SOLUTION

A Key to knowing when faith will be available for you to use

*"Faith will not be yours to use in the service of the Lord until you have **purified your hearts!**"*

Abraham lived too early to hear the words of James 1:6-7. But in that passage, the Apostle, James, encourages the church to **"ask in faith—<u>nothing wavering</u> ...."** Then James describes the life, the emotions and the expectations of that one who is not confident and sure in his faith. He uses the metaphor of a wave that is driven on a storm tossed sea! His conclusion is that the man of wavering faith is ridiculous for imagining that the Lord will advance him anything!

Abraham would have, in all probability, agreed with the learned Apostle, James, when James further states in James 1:8 **that "A double minded man is unstable in all his ways."** Note the instruction in James 4:8, **"Cleanse your hands, ye sinners; and purify your hearts, <u>ye double minded."</u>**

Doubt is a "heart" problem just as faith is a "heart" solution! Cleanse those hands that are ready to do "dirty" and fleshly things in order to accomplish things that a lack of faith will always deny the hopeful. Cleanse those hands that are at the ready to be used as instruments of doubt. And get rid of your double mindedness—you who are unstable in your thinking! Know this! Until your heart is pure and cleansed from every spiritual alloy you will not have singleness of mind! Faith will not be yours to use in the service of the Lord until you have **"purified your hearts!"**

That Abraham did not **"stagger"** is testimony of his pure heart toward his God! The absence of doubt, fear, unbelief and disbelief leaves an emptiness that is ample space for one having **faith *in God's faithfulness!*** All will do well to remember that one of the reasons that God honors faith is—*faith honors God!*

Feathers from the Eagle's Wings

The mind is the thermostat and the body is the thermometer of the man!

CHAPTER 33

———⟫•◦⟪———

DEATH'S GREAT DISDAINER

And being fully persuaded that, what he had promised, he was able also to perform. (Rom. 4:21)

Herein is a key to understanding the Power of God that disdains and has contempt for death.

". . . what . . ." God ". . . had promised He was able to perform!**

"And being fully persuaded . . . ," *Abraham absolutely* **_Knew_!** He was convinced beyond a shadow of doubt! He was *fully persuaded!* What a wonderful freedom it is to have no reservations about both the Ability of your God and His Willingness to answer your prayers! What a powerful measure of commitment is afforded one whose heart is confident to the point that there is no alternative to what one believes is the truth! Abraham could act and speak with unbridled authority because he was categorically positive that ". . . **what** . . ." God ". . . **had promised He was able to perform!** (Rom. 4:21) To the Father of Faith,

(See Rom. 4:11, Rom. 4:16) there was more likelihood of him sprouting wings and flying off to the moon than the likelihood of *him __not__ becoming the father of many nations after God had made him that promise!* **"And being fully persuaded . . . ."** *Abraham absolutely __knew__!*

CHAPTER 34

⸺⸺➤•◈•◄⸺⸺

THE GREAT COMPLAINER

A Key to understanding Paul's great dilemma

I repented—**but my flesh didn't!** *I am saved*—**but my flesh isn't!"**

Rom 7:14 "For we know that the law is spiritual: but I am carnal, sold under sin.

Rom 7:15 For that which I do I allow not: for what I would, that do I not; but what I hate, that do I.

Rom 7:16 If then I do that which I would not, I consent unto the law that *it is* good.

Rom 7:17 Now then it is no more I that do it, but sin that dwelleth in me.

Rom 7:18 For I know that in me (that is, in my flesh,) dwelleth no good thing: for to will is present with me; but *how* to perform that which is good I find not.

Rom 7:19 For the good that I would I do not: but the evil which I would not, that I do.

Rom 7:20 Now if I do that I would not, it is no more I that do it, but sin that dwelleth in me.

Rom 7:21 I find then a law, that, when I would do good, evil is present with me.

Rom 7:22 For I delight in the law of God after the inward man:

Rom 7:23 But I see another law in my members, warring against the law of my mind, and bringing me into captivity to the law of sin which is in my members.

Rom 7:24 O wretched man that I am! who shall deliver me from the body of this death?

Rom 7:25 I thank God through Jesus Christ our Lord. So then with the mind I myself serve the law of God; but with the flesh the law of sin."

Note the uncharacteristic bewailing of that stalwart gladiator for the Faith, the learned Apostle, Paul, in Rom. 7:14-24. There, he who must surely be one of Heaven's favorites (if Heaven has any) complains bitterly! And, he knows with the desperation of one who is aware of his cruel plight with an altogether painful understanding. He knows that, spiritually speaking, he is on Death Row! It is probable that most of those who are on Earth's Death Rows are not hastening death! The learned apostle is no different! He does not want to die! But he knows no way he can live! He is acutely aware that he deserves death but is not ready for justice to be served! Paul complains that the case is stacked against him! It's not fair to him! He did not sign on for this to be his end! But, he has been taught that **sin is recompensed by death!**

Paul has no doubt of the sanctity and the holiness of the Law of God. For he exclaims, **"We know the law is spiritual . . . ."** Truly, **"It's All in _The Knowing!_"** In his spirit, Paul _knows_ **". . . the law is spiritual . . . ."** (Rom. 7:14) Hence, his dilemma is that **" . . . the law is spiritual: <u>but I am carnal . . .</u>! I _am_** flesh and am **<u>of</u>** the flesh! I repented—**but my flesh didn't! I am saved—But my flesh isn't!"**

"And even more than that", says the Apostle, Paul, "I am **". . . sold under sin."** "Without my knowledge and most certainly without my consent—**I am sold under the slavery of sin!** Is there no way out? Is there no spiritual _Under Ground Railroad?_ Is there no divine, _Harriet Tubman_ or _Sojourner Truth_ to spirit me away to freedom? Cannot I (in hope) sing what destiny will prove to be an anthem of freedom to those who will one day be called "People of Color" in years yet to come? Will I qualify to sing that song of victory from oppression, "Free at Last! Free at Last! Thank God Almighty I am Free at Last!?"

The complaint of the Apostle to the Gentiles continues, "I am admittedly out of control! It is almost as if I am of Dissociative Identity Disorder (DID), formerly, called Multiple Personality Disorder (MPD), meaning: having more than one personality! Paul explains further, **"For that which I do I allow not: for what I would, that do I not; but what I hate, that do I."** (Rom 7:15) I am doing what I don't want to do! I sin when I want to live a holy life! Those things that I abhor and am repulsed by are the things that I bring to myself!

The immense problem was that **Paul _Knew_** that he could not escape the responsibility for his sin! We know this to be true because he further declared, **". . . If then I do that which I would not, I consent unto the law that _it is_ good. (**Rom. 7:16) Paul knew that it was his **"consent"** to commit sin that condemned him! Though _his spirit man was resisting the temptation_ and rebelling against every sinful idea—_**in his flesh** he embraced the lusts._ **In his flesh, _Paul approved the lecherous cravings_**_!_

"Now then it is no more I that do it, but sin that dwelleth in me." (Rom 7:17**)** "So," Paul (in earthly wisdom) concludes, "It is not my fault that I sin because it's really not **me** who is doing the damnable thing! It's **my flesh**; my Adamic nature!" Could it be that _there is a way out_ of this morass of accusation and blame; this abyss of condemnation? Could the way out be my excuse that "I really could not help myself?" For, after all, _it is not **me** that God hates!_ **It is _sin_ that God hates!** "Maybe all is not lost!" Paul reasons. "God knows my heart! He knows that my greatest desire is to please Him! God knows that my most heartfelt yearning is, **"That I may know him, and the power of his resurrection, and the fellowship of his sufferings, being made conformable unto his death."** (Php. 3:10) "God knows that I love Him and that I am in this for the duration!"

A Feather from the Eagle's Wings

Your flesh may get you into trouble but don't let you pride keep you there!

CHAPTER 35

IT WASN'T ME OR WAS IT?

In this Chapter is the Key to Understanding who Really Sinned—Paul or the sin in him!

". . . it is no more I that do it, but sin that dwelleth in me."

The great Greek philosopher, Socrates, wisely admonished, *"Know thy self!"* Led by the Holy Spirit, the Apostle, Paul, did not need Socrates to instruct him! He was wise enough to examine himself and learn who and what he was. After studying himself, he announced to all, **". . . I know that in me (that is, in my flesh,) dwelleth no good thing: for to will is present with me; but *how* to perform that which is good I find not.** (Rom 7:18) This man of God knew the good, the bad and the ugly of himself! His introspection showed him that ". . . **in me (that is, in my flesh dwelleth no good thing . . . !"** And he knew that if there was no **"good thing"** in his flesh—there was also no vacancy! Therefore, there was evil and wickedness in his flesh! The proof of that fact was that he could get to the point where he wanted to do right (in his spirit) and he did strive to do right but could not find it in himself (his flesh) to follow through with his righteous intent. Paul always found the classic fight between good and evil being waged in the arena of his mind. **(Rom 7:19) "For the good that I would I do not: but the evil which I would not, that I do."**

Indecisiveness and confusion will always cause one to vacillate and fluctuate between the pro and the con; between the right and the wrong. It is imperative that the Child of God chooses clearly and decidedly what side he is on because—*the middle ground, though too much ground, is no certain ground at all!*

Indecision is the gateway of fools and cowards; fools because they are not wise enough to make any choice (good or bad). Cowards because they know what is right but are not bold enough and convicted enough to make that choice! It is so easy for that person who has no backbone to confer the choice making to someone else and to put the blame on someone else for choices made. Hear now, the Apostle as he muses, "... **if I do that I would not, it is no more I that do it, <u>but sin</u> that <u>dwelleth in me</u>.**" (Rom 7:20) What he is saying is, "Maybe my wrong is not really my fault because after all, it is not really me who am responsible for these wrongs! Could it be that the culprit is really the *"sin that dwelleth in me?"* "Yes," he assures himself, "the true offender is *"the sin that dwelleth in me!"* Perhaps God will not lay the penalty of sin at my doorstep. Surely, I am not really as guilty as it seems?" This new revelation (truly a "Devil-ation") has its basis in a kind of "greasy grace!" "It's not my fault! Paul continues, "I am carnal! I was "**sold under sin**" before I knew what sin was! In the sin and under the curse of First Man (Adam) I was **"sold under sin!"** And, as poor and wretched slaves did their master's will, discounting their own desires—I was sold into that same bondage—but to the cruelest and most heinous slave driver of them all—SIN! It was all a grand setup! The deck was stacked against me from the beginning! How is it my fault that **sin dwelleth in me?"**

His powers of observation and his quick wit agreed, though, with the Spirit of Truth that inspired him to note and record, **"I find then a law that, when I would do good, evil is present with me."** (Rom 7:21) His complaint, like the great patriarch, Job, is **"bitter."** (See Job. 23:2)

". . . When I would do good, evil is present with me." (Rom 7:21) In the quandary of his misery, Paul wonders, "Where do I run and how do I escape an ever present evil? Can I out run myself? I cannot even out distance my shadow! How can I elude my thoughts and evade the desires of my own heart! This ever present evil is so relentless and so persistent that it has become a law of principle and a ruling in my life! Additionally, this law cannot be rescinded, revoked or repealed by any power in the hands of man! Woe is me!"

Further evidence of the contrast between the intents of his spirit and the objectives of his flesh is that Paul states in no uncertain terms, **"For I delight in the law of God after the inward man."** (Rom 7:22) The word, "delight" comes from the Greek word, *"Sunedomai"* which is translated, *"to rejoice in **with oneself**; to feel satisfaction concerning"* and *"to delight."* Paul loves the law of God and rejoices in himself when meditating on the Word. He needs no one to help him lift the name of Jesus and glorify God when he thinks about the Law of God! He feels great satisfaction at the Wonder and the Phenomenon that the Law is! This elation stems from his innermost man; that part of man's entity that deserves the most respect and care—his spirit! Don't forget the parable Jesus told of the rich man who stored up so much of his treasures that he told his soul to, **"take thine ease."** (Luke 12:16-20) God took great umbrage and offense at that! Be careful how you deal with your soul for which Jesus gave the highest measure of devotion! He died for your soul! In his inner man, Paul rejoices with himself at the mention of the Law of God! How wonderful it would be if all men were so devoted to the law, Will and Ways of God!

A Feather from the Eagle's Wings

"God cannot learn because all He could teach Himself is contained in what He knows!"

CHAPTER 36

———✦———

THE BATTLE OF THE WARS

A Key as to why the Battle is Fought and who is winning.

*Paul asks, "Why is the law of my **members**; the law in my flesh—winning?"*

Rom 7:23 "But I see another law in my members, warring against the law of my mind . . . ." After all that was said in verse 22, it seems that Paul is finally on his way to a glorious and unwavering stand for the Law of God. Observe, however, the first word in verse 23. The word is **"But!"** Usually, when you read the word, "but" you can expect a contrast! "He is short but she is tall! He can really eat a lot but she can cook! The word, "but" often precedes a comparison. This time is no different! Paul announces, **". . . I delight in the law of God after the inward man."** He quickly follows with: **"But I see another law in my members . . . ."** Yep, a contrast! I **"delight in the law of God"** but *"I also see another law in my members . . . !"* What I **see** is being viewed by eyes of the flesh and fleshly eyes have satanic sympathies and carnal appetites! How is it fair to use ME against ME! Why cannot the law ***in my mind*** be preeminent in my body? Why can't my spirit man be in control?

What is worse than being in a war is to be in a war that you are losing! The law in my members (my flesh) is WINNING! For, the law in my members is warring against the law of my mind, ***and bringing me into captivity*** to the law of sin which is in my members. What is Paul to believe? What is the truth! Paul had exclaimed in Eph. 4:8(b), God "... **led captivity captive** ... !" In other words, God captured the trap that held us all in bondage! Why then is the law of my **members** ; the law in my flesh—**winning?** Why is the law in my members ***bringing me into captivity*** to the law of sin which is in my members?" I need to ***know!*** And I need to ***know NOW***!

A Feather from the Eagle's Wings

You declare the future who say, "I Can!"

CHAPTER 37

FROM COMPLAINER TO CONQUEROR

In this Chapter there is a Key to "Crying Right"

*Cry tears of grief and even despair if you must
but do it while you seek for, pray for and believe
for—**deliverance!***

"O wretched man that I am!"

(Rom 7:24) Surely, this plaintive cry could not be
the Swan Song of a man such as the Apostle, Paul was!
Certainly, he couldn't go out like that! Such an ignoble end
could not be the finish of such a noble man! The word,
"O" is used almost as a mournful expletive! It explodes out
of his mind and heart, through his mouth and wails into
the atmosphere—just as the pent up anguish and pain of
a bewildered and all but befuddled heart goes the way of
human frailty!

Speaking as one who has a case of the "Can't Help-its,"
he who was **"as one born out of due time," (1Cor. 15:8)**

concludes that despite all of his credentials he is a "wretched man!" Dejected and in abject misery, Paul is at the end of his rope! He is alone and lonely! He is without comfort and can see no end to his plight! He is everything that he detests and has accepted that there is no cure for his malady! As a leper and a pariah, he knows that he doesn't belong in the society that he honors most in his community, the Church of the Living God!

". . . Who shall deliver me from the body of this death? (Rom. 7:24)

Finally, the ion that begged to be asked is uttered! This writer finds it remarkable that Paul's question is not, *"Can* anyone one deliver me and he does not ask *"When?"* or *"How"* will I be delivered!" No! For, he believes that he is beyond redemption now! Forgotten are the truths about the love of God and the Grace that is greater than all our sin! Lost to him are the words that he earlier declared, **". . . where sin abounded, grace did much more abound."** (Rom 5:20) All that he knows is he is a *spiritual undesirable*! His sins are too many to count and too many to overlook! His situation is untenable and without remedy but there is a spark of life in him that says, **"Surely there is Someone who can go my bail! Surely there is Someone who can get me out of this mess!**

One of the worse of life's offerings is the dream that seems futile at the dreaming! Why do we have dreams if there is no way to accomplish them? It must have seemed to the esteemed Apostle that a grand mockery was being perpetrated against him; that his dreaming and even his life are just one grand charade; one colossal hoax at best and a joke that he is the butt of at worse! Again, let us consider the plaintive plea of this would-be stalwart gladiator of the Faith, ". . . Who shall deliver me **from the body** of this death?(Rom. 7:24)

There is something weightier than the *deadness* on his back—there is actually the terrible weight of the **body of death** that bore down on him with ever increasing heaviness! The difference between **the dead** being on Paul and *death* being on him is that *"**dead**" is the condition of one who is not alive* while *"**death**" is **the embodiment of the effects and influences of the state of being dead.** Death is that aspect of life that has the ability to actually bring the living face to face with his or her mortality! Death demands that the living is brought up close and personal with the finality of life by rendering the living—dead! The dead cannot have any effect on the physicality of the living* but (naturally speaking) **the death that is in the dead carries with it gasses that are made of bacteria, odors and germs that can kill the living!** That is the reason we bury our dead six feet under the ground. *We don't need to be protected from the dead **but from the death that is in the dead!***

Death carries with it the stench and the onerous smell of the condemned and the forsaken! Death sometimes seems to tease the living by holding back the dying and causing life to linger! Death off times seems to cause that the living has too much "dead" in him to be alive and yet have too much "life" in him to be dead! Oh, the games that death seems to play! Paul pleads for someone to risk it all for him! He prays for someone to rid him of the reason that no one will care for him. The reason is—*the death that is in his deadness!*

Is there truly no hope? As The Weeping Eyed Prophet, Jeremiah, lamented questioningly, *"Is there* **no balm in Gilead"** to heal the sin sick soul? (Jer. 8:22) *"Is there* **no physician there?"** Here, Jeremiah is keening and bemoaning what he believes is the hopeless plight of his people. They are sin sick and there is no indication of a ready cure for them. Being fully aware of his location and that at Gilead people had always found healing herbs to apply to their wounds, he wonders that his people continue to be sick. The presence of physicians was usually in evidence in Gilead as they came regularly to harvest plants for healing salves, poultices and powders. But there was certainly no cure for sin sickness outside of the Love and Mercy of God!

"O wretched man that I am! who shall deliver me from the body of this death?" (Rom. 7:24) The piteous and heart wrenching cry escapes his lips in a moment of terrible and extreme despair. Surely, despite the fact that Paul cannot come up with the answer to this painful question, the Lord of Mercy and Grace has a Plan!

Fully aware that what he needs is not *something to make him feel better about what is making him feel worse,* Paul prays for a deliverer! He doesn't want a temporary fix! He doesn't pray for a bandage! Paul wants a cure that will be so complete and so permanent that he will never be able to be damaged in this way again! He wants deliverance from the strength that has left him so weak! He wants to be completely extricated from his dilemma! Somehow, Paul perceives that it will be a Someone and not a thing that will rescue him! So, he queries, ". . . **WHO shall deliver me . . . ?"** (Rom. 7:24)

If I could beg an audience with the great Apostle, Paul, I would remind him even as I bring you, my dear student of biblical truth, into remembrance of Jesus' experience when no one supported Him! This was when everyone, including His inner circle, distanced themselves from Him and Peter began ". . . **to curse and to swear,** *saying,* **I know not the man.**" (Mat 26:74) This was Peter's vain effort to demonstrate to all that he was not one of Jesus' followers! Well, Jesus experienced that aloneness to a degree that was far, far greater than anyone had ever experienced before! For, when He hanged on the cruel and mean Cross of Calvary, He was assuredly a man without relations and friends; a man without a country and worse still, he was—**a man without a God!** There is no more lonely a plight than that! This was far more terrible than even He knew it would be!

Observe, we heard nothing from Him in defense of Himself as He was dragged from judgment hall to judgment hall to be lied on, persecuted and tortured! In fact, "**He was oppressed, and he was afflicted, yet he opened not his mouth: he is brought as a lamb to the slaughter, and as a sheep before her shearers is dumb, so he openeth not his mouth.**

(Isa 53:7) No! Paul, the Lamb of God did not make a sound! He suffered through all that He endured! And He did it *with His mother ever present—but He was just out of the reach of her gentle touch and care!* The **man,** Jesus, had to distance Himself from his earthly mother for he had to become her earthly sacrifice! He also had to remain separate from her because he knew that in her years to come—she would need a God and she would need to be able to come to Him! He had already promised, **"I go to prepare a place for you that where I am there ye may be also!"** But what a heartless mockery Mary's presence must have been to her son; to the baby she suffered ostracisms and stigmas for because she bore Him out of wedlock! His mother was so near as to be able to see and count every tear that lapped down His face. She was close to enough hear His labored and raspy breathing as His parched and raw throat stung and burned from the vinegar and the gall His torturers gave Him to drink! *But she could not reach Him!* His ever faithful mother was so near to Him and yet *she was a whole world away from Him!*

But, we heard no complaint from Him, Children of God, as He made those preparations! *We heard nothing from Him!* He had to look upon bestial and animalistic people as they looked and leered at Him and jeered His naked form. He heard them make their lewd remarks and He despised the shame that would have filled those who had a lesser love; those who would have given in to the decency and honor of their noble and dignified character—but this One—*He made no sound! !*

Oh, beloved Apostle, Paul, by my rehearsing the sufferings of our Lord, I am not to any degree seeking to make less of the pain that wracked your mind! I know that your tears were hot and briny! I know your pain was your own pain! But, dear Paul, I would give anything if you could know this and be comforted by it—*the tears you cried—Jesus cried them first!* And I want all of you, my weeping readers, to have *The Knowing* that any mental anguish you know—*He knew first!* You have not shed one tear truly alone or endure one iota of discomfort by yourself—*Jesus was there!* *And He was there first!*

But hear the Christ, now, Paul, as He is impaled on that callous and pitiless tree and for the first time in His life He experiences total and absolute aloneness! See the unimaginable sadness in his eyes of Love, all of you suffering readers, when the searing pain of *the sin that He became* touches Him; changes Him; mutates Him! **"For he hath made him to be sin for us, who knew no sin ; that we might be made the righteousness of God in him."** (2 Cor. 5:21 KJV) See him morph and change before your mind's eye as He becomes the sin of the world; as He becomes the liar's lie, the murderer's murder and the adulterer's act of adultery! See Him transformed when sins upon sins; all of the sins of the world are heaped on Him until He becomes a grotesque caricature of His former self! See Jesus as He becomes the shame and the transgression of all those before Him all the way back to Adam! See Him also as He becomes all of the sins that would ever be committed in His future even until the rapture of the church! See Him become the sins upon sins that are amassed and piled on Him rendering Him **". . . without form or comeliness!"** (Isa. 53:2) But, all must Know beyond any shadow of doubt that *Jesus did not become a sinner!* *He became the sins that sinners committed!**

Be witness, dear Student-of-the-Truth, be witness with the Apostle, Paul, as now the hurt caused by *the world's greatest betrayal* slashes and tears away at His mind; driving His peace completely out of His world and threatening His very sanity! Yes, Paul, I did say, *"the world's greatest betrayal!"* For, after all of humanity forsook Him, the

IT'S ALL IN THE KNOWING

supreme treachery was—**His Own Father's "betrayal!"** Listen, Paul, with your mind's ear and hear the shout that reached the portals of Heaven! Give ear, you Saints of the Most High God and hear the sound that caused the Devil and all of his demons to shriek and to howl in fiendish delight! He stilled the voice of chaos in the lives of many! He quelled the storms that threatened the very futures of so many lives! He lifted massive burdens from the hearts of many whose dreams were being crushed! And to those who experienced living nightmares He gave dreams and visions! But now, Paul and you, Dear Reader, listen to the pitiful cry of the Prince of Peace as He seeks vainly for an answer to the unanswerable question, ". . . **Eli, Eli, lama sabachthani? that is to say, My God, my God, why hast thou forsaken me?"** (Mat 27:46) Yes, Paul, hear Him cry out and know that while you groan and travail in your dire circumstances, laboring under the unforgiving weight of the (See Rom. 7:24) ". . . **body of this death,"** you Paul, *are in the best of company!*

Christ Jesus had ample reasons for His feelings of disillusionment and confusion. There was certainly a foundation for His sentiments of betrayal and disenfranchisement because:

- ❖ His Own Father gave the impression in the Garden of Gethsemane that He was in full support of His Son, Jesus, by sending the angels to strengthen Him! afterward His Own Father forsook Him!
- ❖ It even ". . . **pleased the Lord to bruise him."** Isa **53:10 KJV**

❖ His Own Father turned Him over to His enemies and at the moment of the torture seemed to have no plan or interest in saving Him from their clutches!

❖ His Own Father permitted Satan and all of his demons to have Him in all of their diabolical pleasures!

❖ He knew that His Father hated sin more than anything else and yet His Father made Jesus become that hated sin!

❖ **For he hath made him *to be* sin for us, who knew no sin . . . ."** Co 5:21

❖ Jesus, the poster child for all that is righteous and holy, had to deal with something worse than committing sin—**He actually became sin *personified!***

Yes, they heard Jesus cry out for His Father and He cried out understandably and justifiably! Therefore, Saints of God, Paul was not to be blamed for succumbing to the fears, frustrations and the pain of his ordeal! This writer says, "Cry if you must! But only for the right reasons! Cry tears of grief and even despair *if you must* but do it *while you seek for, pray for and believe for—deliverance!*

A Feather from the Eagle's Wings

Don't let you "Old Man" mock your "New Man!"

CHAPTER 38

———⇒•◦•⇐———

DO YOU REALLY *KNOW* YOU?

A Key to the Identity of the Paul in this Chapter

But, what things were gain to me, those I counted loss
for Christ. (Phil. 3:7)

Php. 3:4   **Though I might also have confidence in the
flesh. If any other man thinketh that he hath whereof
he might trust in the flesh, I more:**

Php 3:5   **Circumcised the eighth day, of the stock of
Israel, *of* the tribe of Benjamin, an Hebrew of the
Hebrews; as touching the law, a Pharisee;**

Php 3:6   **Concerning zeal, persecuting the church;
touching the righteousness which is in the law,
blameless.**

Php 3:7   **But, what things were gain to me, those I
counted loss for Christ.**

Php 3:8 **Yea, doubtless, and I count all things *but* loss for the excellency of the knowledge of Christ Jesus my Lord: for whom I have suffered the loss of all things, and do count them *but* dung, that I may win Christ . . . .**

Phil. 3:4-6 depicts a much different Paul than the *"wretched man"* that Paul sees himself to be in Rom. 7:14-25. The Paul that is seen in Romans chapter 7 is far removed from the credentials that he deservedly wore in the epistle to the Philippians.

"Though, I might also have confidence in the flesh. If any other man thinketh that he hath whereof he might trust in the flesh, I more . . . ." (Phil. 3:4)

Speaking from the vantage point of strength, his confidence in his identity comes through loud and clear. "I," Paul seems to say, "even as others who blow their own horns am able to have confidence in who I am! Bring them on," he challenges, "who feel that they have reasons to boast in themselves—*because I have the greatest of proofs of my worthiness!* Here is no weeping, wailing, plaintive voice of a defeated man! Here we find the voice of a man fully vested in his God and is clothed in full spiritual regalia! He is spiritually confident, having disdain for the temporal and earthly. He has much of earth's trappings that he could revel in concerning his national and spiritual treasures of honor and prestige! But all of these he counted ". . . **loss for the excellency of the knowledge of Christ Jesus**" and "***but* dung, that I may win Christ**"

Be reminded, Dear Reader, of the time in his life when Paul was mistaken by a captain of the Roman army for an Ethiopian who caused great chaos and confusion in Jerusalem and ultimately helped four thousand men who were murderers escape into the wilderness. He knew that he had to be very convincing as he defended himself to the captain and to those Jews who sought to kill him. See, here, his defense:

- ○ **I am verily a man** *which am* **a Jew,**
- ○ **born in Tarsus,** *a city* **in Cilicia,**
- ○ **yet brought up in this city at the feet of Gamaliel,** *and*
- ○ **taught according to the perfect manner of the law of the fathers,**
- ○ **and was zealous toward God, as ye all are this day.** Act 22:3

❖ **Though, I might also have confidence in the flesh. If any other man thinketh that he hath whereof he might trust in the flesh, I more . . . . Circumcised the eighth day,**

- ○ Paul was circumcised the eighth day after his birth which was according to the law of God.

- ○ After his conversion and his New Birth, he was faithful to both the Church and the covenant that God had with Israel!

❖ **of the stock of Israel,**

    ○ He was not a new comer or a proselyte to the Chosen Children of God but was born into that lineage,

❖ **of the tribe of Benjamin,**

    ○ Paul was a son of the "favorite" son, Benjamin,

    ○ He was of the tribe that stood faithful and dedicated to Judah when the other tribes rebelled.

    ○ He was, incidentally, of the tribe the Temple stood in.

❖ **an Hebrew of the Hebrews**

    ○ His father was a Hebrew (Jew)

    ○ His mother was a Hebrew (Jew)

    ○ None of his ancestry had ever married a Gentile!

    ○ Paul was also a Roman citizen because he was born in the Roman province of Cilicia

❖ **As touching the law a Pharisee.**

    ○ Having sat at the feet of one of the most prominent educators of the law in that day,

Gamaliel, Paul indeed was a Pharisee. (Acts 22:3)

o In every respect of Jewish teaching Paul excelled so that he knew every nuance and norm of Jewish culture and the laws of his fathers.

o Like his father, Paul was a Pharisee

o The Pharisee was the most exacting and strict faction of the Jewish society and Paul was one of them.

❖ **Concerning zeal, persecuting the church**

At this time in Paul's life he could readily compare himself to the characterization that he gave Israel in Rom. 10:2-3

"Brethren, my heart's desire and prayer to God for Israel is, that they might be saved."

❖ **Rom 10:2 For I bear them record that they have a zeal of God, but not according to knowledge.**
❖ **Rom 10:3 For they being ignorant of God's righteousness, and going about to establish their own righteousness, have not submitted themselves unto the righteousness of God.**
❖ **Concerning zeal, persecuting the church**

o Paul's heart was in the right place but **his head was not!**

○ For he did not realize that he was waging war against the very same God that he thought he was defending.

Note Paul's defense to the Jews concerning those who sought to kill him at Jerusalem:

❖ Acts 22(b) **I . . . was zealous toward God, <u>as ye all are this day.</u>**

○ <u>**Perhaps it's his training at the feet of one of the premier lawyers of his day, Gamaliel that gave him this defense to their accusations.**</u>

○ He countered, "My zeal **is no different than yours** this day!"

▪ Act 22:4 **And <u>I persecuted this way unto the death,</u> binding and delivering into prisons both men and women.**

▪ Act 22:5**As also the high priest doth bear me witness, and all the estate of the elders: from whom also I received letters unto the brethren, and went to Damascus, to bring them which were there bound unto Jerusalem, for to be punished.**

○ Blameless though Paul was—*he was not perfect!*

215

- **I persecuted this way unto the death, binding and delivering into prisons both men and women.**

  O Paul was in no way one to sit around wondering, "What's going on!" He was always in the thick of it!

  O True to his beliefs, Paul was a very active activist **"for God!"**

    • He was dedicated to his God—to a fault!

    • He even **"received letters unto the brethren, and went to Damascus, to bring them which were there bound unto Jerusalem, for to be punished."**

Acts 22:5(c) As also the high priest doth bear me witness, and all the estate of the elders: from whom also I received letters unto the brethren.

  ❖ The High Priest and all of the elders were called on for a witness to Paul's walk as a most excellent Jew.

  ❖ But it was no less a personage than Jesus, the Christ, Who said, **"And when they bring you unto the synagogues, and *unto* magistrates, and powers, take ye no thought how or what thing ye shall answer, or what ye shall say:**

(Luk 12:12) For the Holy Ghost shall teach you in the same hour what ye ought to say." (Luk. 12:11)

○ How can they not know that Paul is a good and faithful Jew? They gave him the documents to be used in killing, imprisoning and punishing the Christians!

○ Are they not under condemnation who give authority to blasphemers and seditionists who **"teacheth all men everywhere against the people, and the law, and this place, and hath polluted this holy place?"**

The apostle to the gentiles did not know *while he was persecuting the Church* that he was destined to say, ". . . **the natural man receiveth not the things of the Spirit of God: for they are foolishness unto him: neither can he know** *them,* **because they are spiritually discerned.** When Paul was wreaking havoc on the Christian Church he knew nothing about the flesh and the spirit, the law of sin and true Holiness! He did not realize it but despite his piety and his religiosity **he was living in his flesh!** AND BECAUSE HE WAS NOT HOLY SPIRIT DRIVEN *there was no way that he could understand the real issues!*

A Feather from the Eagle's Wings

*"Because God is love He never has to decide **to love** but He does have to **decide not to love!**"*

CHAPTER 39

MOVED BY THE HAND OF GOD

**Eze 37:1 The hand of the LORD was upon me,
and carried me out in the spirit of the LORD,
and set me down in the midst of the valley which
was full of bones.**

A Key to the Phenomenon . . . that will . . . beat all Life's Phenomenon is in this Chapter.

Abraham's age and the fact of his body, **"now dead,"** and Sarah being so far past the flowering of her age that the **"deadness"** of her body was worth mentioning in Holy Scripture *placed them in very good company.* For the Prophet, Ezekiel had a most unique and memorable experience dealing with God as death's "Great Disdainer." It really should be no great marvel that Life would hold death in disdain, contempt and disregard! However, Ezekiel is not God! And death had been the most formidable opponent that man has ever faced! Everybody Ezekiel knew who died—**stayed dead**! But please read this saga in its entirety and consider the phenomenon to beat all his life's phenomenon!

Never doubt the lengths that the Lord will go to in order to accomplish His agenda! Ezekiel was fully surrendered to the Spirit of God when he had a vision! Jehovah God *could have* merely instructed the obedient prophet to go to the valley just as He told Ezekiel to go to the "plain" in Ezek. 3:22. For we find in Ezek. 3:22" **The hand of the Lord was upon me there, and he said to me, "Get up and go out to the plain, and there I will speak to you."**

Instead of God exercising His Divine Authority and simply commanding the prophet to **"Get up and go"** it is recorded, **"But Ezekiel was ". . . carried . . . out in the Spirit of the Lord . . . and set . . . down in the midst of the valley which was full of bones."**

Don't let the fact that the valley was **"full of bones"** give the impression that the bones were indiscriminately amassed in a great pile that spread across the valley. These bones were not haphazardly thrown in a heap or placed very neatly on top of one another as if in preparation burial. These bones were, for the most part, in configurations of placement that declared that they had fallen in battle. They were, in all probability, in very much the same place they were when they fell. It is likely that the head lay next to or above the neck bones that lay in their expected places near the clavicle and so on. Picture, if you will the fatal arrow, spear, sword or the dagger that took the life—lying near the bones of each warrior.

These bones lay unburied in an open valley! Why did none of the families and loved ones of the dead come to find their remains? Why were they left exposed to the elements and for so long that the bones were **"very dry!"**

There are those today who question as to why God left the broken "bones" of their failures out in public view for the world to see. There are still others who wonder if the signs and the evidences of their misdoings were left in full view of the world just so the wrongdoers could be treated as pariahs to be avoided at all costs! Then, what of those who in their darkest moments believe that God left the gaping wounds of their sin and shame exposed to the view of gossip mongers, talebearers and false judges *to be reminders to themselves* that of all the earth—*they are the scum?* What of others who are hapless victims of their own fleshly desires and wonder if the "bones" of their broken dreams were left to be viewed by an unjust and unfeeling humanity simply so that all would know what could happen to them should they ever be so weak, careless and imperfect as to presumptuously fail a Perfect God!

But what of the innocent ones who are the victims of Satan's evil strategies? Those who were not guilty but could not prove they were not guilty? And what of those who **"chose to suffer afflictions with the people of God than to enjoy the pleasures of sin for a season . . . ?"** **(Heb. 11:25)** And finally, let us not forget those that gave the highest measure of devotion and sacrificed their lives because they **". . . loved not their lives unto the death."** **(Rev. 12:11)** Why were their "bones" left in the open? Those "bones" are affidavits of the Blood Bought devotees and their selfless loyalty. Those "bones" are the hallmark of every true believer. These martyrs are also indictments to the villainous, cowardly and sinful hordes that chose sin over righteousness and lowly living over the lofty and holy ideals of the Living God! These gave the highest measure of devotion (their lives) for the cause of Christ!

Perhaps the true reason God left the bones unburied was to give the hope of resurrection! Possibly, it was God's intent that those bones silently scream to all who are believers that *God can have a plan for them even after they have failed Him in the worst of ways* and after they have been thrown away by their closest and staunchest supporters! Maybe the bones serve to say that *what has been can, by the Grace of God, be once again—<u>even after they have given up on themselves;</u>* long after the "bones" of their dreams have died and—***even after their death***!

A Feather from the Eagle's Wings

"If you have hope you can cope!"

CHAPTER 40

――――►♦◄――――

BONES TOO DEAD, BONES TOO DRY

Eze 37:2And caused me to pass by them round about: and, behold, *there were* very many in the open valley; and, lo, *they were* very dry.

"A Key that Reaffirms the Power of God Over the Things that are Most Dead."

Sometimes, it is not only the thing that happens that promises something will be a "God Thing." Rather, often times the circumstances that prevail declare that God is about to "bust a move!" Note that God *refused* to defend this army. He refused to keep it alive and victorious with His Omnipotence and by His Omniscience and by doing so He denied this army the celebration and the praise worthy heroics that are the hallmark of an indefatigable, relentless and conquering defense force. The All Knowing and Compassionate Mind of God allowed the loss of whatever the trophies were that would have been the booty and the prize of the win should the army have been victorious! Somehow, **this <u>must</u> be a "God Thing!"**

There are always the benefits that would have been enjoyed if the army had been successful but there are also the costs and the penalties to be borne when failure to win the battle is experienced! Before the war began, God knew that the army would be defeated! Before the war started Divine Wisdom decreed the loss! Throughout time the annals of history have recorded that God has caused military forces that were sorely outnumbered and outgunned to triumph against seeming impossible odds! But never since the beginning of time has He purposely orchestrated at best or permitted at the very least the defeat of an entire army for the purpose of declaring to the entire world His supremacy over death, hell and the grave! Never had God built a stage of this magnitude to announce to the world that until God speaks His unimpeachable and infallible Word, **hope is never truly hopeless**! And *until God "gives up," positive possibility* **never needs surrender to impossibility;** *"can"* **is never at the mercy of** *"can't"* **and** *"final"* **is never to be swallowed up by "finality!!"** From this day forward the world can be gladden by the reality that the Power of God is an All Prevailing Force! The Will of God is the Ultimate Authority and the Name of God is an All Encompassing Solution!

How did a just and loving God determine that an entire army, as a dispensable pawn, will know the agony of defeat and pay the highest measure of devotion? Will an entire army of stalwart gladiators be sacrificed just so that the Lord of All can come back into His world and intervene at a time when every logic and truth on Earth knows that *it is too late?* But, somehow, the Heart of God knew that the greater good would be known if man's agenda were thwarted in favor of Divine Agenda!

What was the hope of the battle? Who are they whom God loves and whose lives would have been bettered if the crusade had been won? Who died not receiving the advantages and the gains that was their hearts desires; never realizing the fruition of their vision? Who were they whose loved ones never came home from the war?

Then, who were the enemies that should have been overthrown and subjugated and would have had it not been for the intervention of Divine Agenda? Did they know that they really did not win the battle except by default and forfeiture? Did they know the great sacrifice that was made that they would not experience utter annihilation? Did they give God the glory? Whether they did or not it really doesn't matter because God was not after a mediocre, mundane, tedious or commonplace praise. God wanted and deserved *maximum glory!*

Led by the Spirit of God, Ezekiel inspected the bones. Close examination showed that they were there in abundance and they were "... **very dry.**" Nowhere in the scriptures is there found a more dismal and bleak characterization of a situation! The bones were *"very dry."* The bones were not merely dead (which would have been bad enough) they *were even more than dry!* They were *"very dry!"* They were more than dead! They were *"very dry;"* <u>*very dead!*</u> So, it appears that there are degrees of deadness **and potentials for reliving** and <u>**these bones were far past that hope !**</u> Resuscitation is possible if the body is newly dead. But what are the odds if the marrow of the bones has dried up? What is brought to the table when _**very dry**_ bones are all there is to work with? It is said that where there is life—there is hope! However, these bones were past hoping for.

CHAPTER 41

IT'S STILL IN *THE KNOWING*

A Key to the Real Question that God Asked Ezekiel is in this Chapter

"Ezekiel cared more about giving an answer than he did about understanding the question!"

Eze 37:3 And he said unto me, Son of man, can these bones live? And I answered, O Lord GOD, thou knowest.

When pressed for an answered as to whether the bones can live, the prophet knew his answer and he gave it, "Thou knowest!" Ezekiel knew that He was safe giving that reply. For it was the truth! The All *Knowing* God knew the answer! If the words had been designed to trap him—Ezekiel was safe! If he really didn't know the specific answer—he was safe—for *the truth is ample cover* because as Jesus was destined to say, **"Ye shall know the truth, and the truth shall make you free." (John 8:32)**

Despite those truths, God was giving the Prophet an opportunity to emphasize and glorify the Power of God. Remember, Dear Ones, the question was not in reference to Ezekiel's abilities or the lack thereof. "Can these bones live? The inference is "Can these bones live—*by any means?*" How often has God posed a similar puzzle to we who are called by His name today? What we have often seen as an impossible challenge would never have been perceived in that negative light had we considered that there is nothing too hard for the Lord! All too often, instead of us looking to the inexhaustible Power and Mind of God—we examine issues by human logic and never ascribe to God the definition of What He truly is—The Almighty God!

When Jehovah called Ezekiel, **"Son of man,"** He was making Ezekiel to know that He was perfectly aware of Ezekiel's weakness and the finite scope of his intelligence. Now, God never asks stupid and ridiculous questions. The very nature of the question should have gotten Ezekiel's interest. But just as we so often do, Ezekiel cared more about giving an answer than he did about understanding the question! Remember this, my friend, the *answer to most questions in life is usually found in completely understanding the question!* For instance, if I say, Where is the place that you can always find here but you can never find there! What comes to your mind? Do you start thinking of geographical locations or situations? Actually, neither of those ideas will afford you the proper thinking. You see, I didn't ask a question at all. I made a statement. See it again: *"Where" is the place you can always find "here" but you can never find there!"* *"Where"* is the place that you will always fine *"here"* because the word, *"here"* is a part of the spelling of the word, *"where!"*

If Ezekiel had studied the question, the answer would have appeared in a flash! Question: "Can these bones live?" Answer: "Lord, with You all things are possible!" Yes, the Prophet gave the safe answer **and he was not wrong *but he could have given a more complete answer!*** The answer that he gave did not require, suggest or expect any action from God. God always wants His Children to call Him to action!

CHAPTER 42

PROPHESY *FOR ALL WHO HAVE NO VOICE*—BELIEVE *FOR ALL WHO HAVE NO HEART*

A Key to what we must do for our "Dry Bones."

Be preemptive! Take authority and decree the salvation of your loved ones!

Eze 37:4 Again he said unto me, Prophesy upon these bones, and say unto them, O ye dry bones, hear the word of the LORD.

One of the most powerful of all human interventions that was recorded in scripture is found in this episode in the life of Ezekiel. Pay strict attention to the divine command. **"Ezekiel, prophesy *upon* these bones ...."** Most prophesy is spoken to or about someone. That cannot work here for these bones are dead, remember? They are *dry* and **very** dry at that! They cannot hear Ezekiel's voice! They cannot respond of their own accord!

In much the same way, there are probably *"dry bones"* in your life. These "Dry Bones" are people in whose heart there no spiritual life and no desire to live for God! You can talk to these people until you are blue in the face but these "Dry bones" will never respond to any overtures you make toward their salvation! You can't feed one who is not hungry—you will just choke him! You must do as Eliphaz the Temanite promised Job, **"Thou shalt also decree a thing, and it shall be established unto thee: and the light shall shine upon thy ways."** (Job 22:28) Be preemptive! Take authority and decree the salvation of your loved one **". . . and it shall be established unto thee . . . ."** You will pronounce salvation for you loved ones and the Lord shall establish it in the Earth and record it in Heaven. For, **". . . the light shall shine upon thy ways."** One rendering of the word, **"light"** as it is translated from the Hebrew is, *"happiness."* God will assure you happiness and that joy will be caused by the perfect accomplishing of your decree.

So, Ezekiel was not told to address the bones! Rather God instructed him to prophesy *in their regard.* It was not the bone's understanding, agreement or their willingness to follow the plan that would affect this miracle! It was the man of God's obedience to the Word of God that was the key!

How often has the Holy Spirit instructed His Saints to pray for those who were not able to see God's purpose for their lives (because of the thickness of the scales on their eyes?) How many are the times when God has told me to utter powerful life giving words over the lives of those whose hearts are dead to the voice and the unction of the Holy Spirit? When you speak God's Word *at God's unction*—God takes control and achieves the victory! Those "Dry Bones" of missed opportunities, seemingly forgotten promises of God, destroyed relationships, good intentions gone bad etc.—SHALL LIVE!

CHAPTER 43

BREATHING HIS BREATH

A Key to Knowing how and why God put breath in the "very dry" bones is in this chapter.

"... nothing can live without breathing His Breath!"

Eze 37:5 Thus saith the Lord GOD unto these bones; Behold, I will cause breath to enter into you, and ye shall live:

It is a misnomer; it is not a full and complete statement to say that God *has* life. For, He *is* life and the very source of it! He is the Power and the Life of life. God is the Reality of life! He is the Concept of life and He is the Essence of life! The Fundamental Nature of Life (God) always leaves a residue of Himself wherever He is. And He is, ultimately, (speaking spiritually) *"... the Life." (Joh.11:25)*

Divine Thought had purposed that these bones live! So, it follows that God Himself (Life) will ensure that the bones have breath. All breath, all wind is from God!

Whether the breath has its origin in the Mouth of God or should the wind be the consequence of the Infallible Will of God—**all breath; all wind is of God!** *And nothing can live without breathing His Breath!* **"And the LORD God formed man** *of* **the dust of the ground, and** <u>**breathed into his nostrils the breath of life**</u>**; and man** <u>**became a living soul.**</u>**"** (Gen 2:7)

What more certain way can there be for God to **"...cause breath to enter** ... the very dry bones than for the God of that purpose to intervene and breathe **upon** those bones as He breathed **into** the nostrils of First Man? So, because the bones had no nostrils, God purposed to breathe **upon** the bones! And He declared *with all the Power, Might and Certainty that He is,* **"And ye shall live."**

What a promise! What a hope! "Ye shall live!" Despite your present condition; regardless of what the predictors and prognosticators say, "Ye shall live!" *It doesn't matter how long* ***your life had been dead***, <u>***"Ye shall live!"***</u> They may say that you are too old, to sick or even too dead to live but—**<u>YOU SHALL LIVE!</u>**

A Feather from the Eagle's Wings

*"To listen and hear God <u>when He is silent</u> is one of the greatest signs of our trust in Him! When we know how very much He loves us, <u>we can hear (in our spirit) the sound of His Love working for us</u>—**even in His silence!**"*

CHAPTER 44

———⊷•⊷———

"I WILL DO" AND "YE SHALL KNOW!"

In this Chapter is a Key that will unlock the mystery of—"The Miracle in the Valley of Dry Bones!"

"God said, I will—that you may know!"

Eze 37:6 **And I will lay sinews upon you, and will bring up flesh upon you, and cover you with skin, and put breath in you, and ye shall live; and ye shall know that I *am* the LORD.**

Everything that God does on Earth will affect His masterpiece (man) in some way. Most assuredly, when God announces His *intentions for man* and the benefits of those *intentions to man* there is a certainty of *influence on man*. *Everything that God does to effect a change in man's life should teach man something about the Creator that will afford man the opportunity to become something he has never been.* In the scenario of this verse God promises to provide the sinews, flesh and skin and the breath for each skeletal

237

frame. Our Father is the All Sufficient God! He plans for the completion of His Will! God did not just speak His Word and create another army as He spoke His Word when He made the world in the beginning! He didn't start all over from Scratch! He used the same physical infrastructure (the now very dry bones) and represented this army to the world. This symbolized that He was Master over the dead and death, Lover to those on the other side of death and Re-creator of His Own creation!

It must also be said that God is not satisfied with the mere *existence of things*! He requires that ***everything that has potential reach that potential!*** Please note: He had a valley full of bones that used to be men. The Father is never gratified until potentials are realized; until possibilities have become realities and destinies are fulfilled. So, a valley of ***"dry bones"*** is a clarion call to arms for the Creator of Worlds! Given the Nature of God, as much as I am aware of it, Divine Intervention in that valley was simply a matter of time! And God said, "*...I will*—**and** *you may know* ...!" Is it amazing to you, my dear student, that God did all of this so that a dead army; a multitude of **"very dry"** bones will one day know that even in their wasted and undone condition—**our God is their God?!**

I wonder how often the children of God have questioned the wait, the delay and the seeming denial of the answer to their prayers! These questionings occurred because God's Children did not always *know* that though they could not see the busyness of our Father, God, in the times of what they labeled "delay" and "denial," *He was building the infrastructure* that is the foundation needed for the supplying of our need; our desires; our futures; our lives!

In our rush to enjoy the finished product we may oft times miss the most exquisite miracle of the entire process—THE PROCESS! For we all too frequently find ourselves most impatient with Divine Timing!

In this passage of scripture, we receive a great lesson on how to plan and provide for our own lives. God did everything in raising these bones from the dead that we need to do to build anything in life!

❖ He had divine purpose for His miracle!
❖ He had a plan.
❖ He was the Power and the Resources and
❖ He recorded the plan (in the heart and mind of the prophet) and
❖ He executed His Plan!

"And ye shall <u>know</u> that I am the Lord."

Perhaps in their life time they did not learn to honor Our Lord as God! It is so like the Love of God to love them, forgive them and provide for them another chance to **know** Him—even after they had been long dead! It's still *"All in The Knowing!*

Joh 20:24 But Thomas, one of the twelve, called Didymus, was not with them when Jesus came.

Joh 20:25 The other disciples therefore said unto him, We have seen the Lord. But he said unto them, Except I shall see in his hands the print of the nails, and put my finger into the print of the nails, and thrust my hand into his side, I will not believe.

Joh 20:26 And after eight days again his disciples were within, and Thomas with them: *then* **came Jesus, the doors being shut, and stood in the midst, and said, Peace** *be* **unto you.**

Joh 20:27 Then saith he to Thomas, Reach hither thy finger, and behold my hands; and reach hither thy hand, and thrust *it* **into my side: and be not faithless, but believing.**

Joh 20:28 And Thomas answered and said unto him, My Lord and my God.

Joh 20:29 Jesus saith unto him, Thomas, because thou hast seen me, thou hast +believed: blessed *are* **they that have not seen, and** *yet* **have believed.**

The spirit of Thomas (who was called, Didymus—meaning, "Twin") is, unfortunately, alive and well! That spirit is called, *"a doubting spirit!"* Thomas was with Jesus and the rest of the disciples when miracles were wrought at the command of the Christ. He was in their number when the Son of God manifested Himself as God in a Body!

Psa 135:15 The idols of the heathen *are* **silver and gold, the work of men's hands.**

Psa 135:16 They have mouths, but they speak not; eyes have they, but they see not;

Psa 135:17 They have ears, but they hear not; neither is there *any* **breath in their mouths.**

Psa 135:18 They that make them are like unto them: *so is* every one that trusteth in them.

When men make their gods, whether of silver and gold as many heathen do or when they fashion them from the clay of logic and reason as did Thomas, **"They that make them are like unto them: *so is* every one that trusteth in them. They have mouths, but they speak not ..."** the truth of the Word of God! "... **Eyes have they, <u>but they see not ...</u>"** heaven's realities **<u>when they are staring them in the face!</u> "They have mouths, but they speak not ..."** those things that glorify God as God but, in the vanity of their minds, they worship their own finite understanding. And, **"They have ears, but they hear not ..."** the Voice of their Creator!

Yes! Perhaps somewhere in the Divine Plan was the Grace that would give these warriors whose bones had become very dry another chance; another opportunity to speak for the God of their new life! Never forget that God Knew with copious clarity the identity of these fallen ones! Maybe this unprecedented act of Grace would offer these whose names were swallowed up in eternity the chance to focus and to see what they were too distracted to set their eyes on! Could it really be that the Love of God so favored these soldiers that they would have one more time to stop and listen to Words from the Loving Heart of our Loving God that they may have ignored all of the time of their former lives? **He Knew intimately each soul that had paid the highest measure of devotion and <u>God cared!</u>** Keep reading, Dear Reader, don't stop studying this book and you will *Know* who these chosen ones were!

CHAPTER 45

CONFUSION PRECEDES ORDER AND CLARITY

An amazing Key that celebrates the power and the blessedness of obedience is in this chapter.

"When you obey God—look for a change; any change!"

Eze 37:7 So I prophesied as I was commanded: and as I prophesied, there was a noise, and behold a shaking, and the bones came together, bone to his bone.

Before planting there must be plowing! Before soothing and healing there must be pain and sickness. Before God brought order to this valley of dry bones there was chaos and the sounds of confusion! However, before the momentous occasion of this miraculous phenomenon, birds sang in the Valley of Dry Bones. The winds rustled through the leafy boughs of trees that were planted by the Hand of God! Until the Valley was disturbed by the Awesome Power of the Living God, as He gave Life, the only sounds that were heard in that valley were the natural sounds of one of

Nature's valleys! Heard in the valley of dry bones was the lonely hoot of the night owl, the chattering of squirrels as they raced one another to the next crisp and succulent nut and perhaps the musical sound of a cascading waterfall. But now, the great Commander in Chief of all Commanders in Chiefs gives His fateful order to Ezekiel and " . . . **there was a noise, and behold a shaking, and the bones came together, bone to his bone.**"

Ezekiel obeyed God! That was his duty; a duty required by the Giver of the command! It must be clearly understood that faith required nothing less than an obedient response; and the believer could do no less! When you obey God—look for a change; any change! For, that change is evidence that God is busy!

The story was told to me of an episode that was purported to have taken place in the life of Christopher Columbus. The three ships under his command: the Nina, the Pinta and the Santa Maria were lost and had been lost on the ocean for months! One day Captain Columbus called one of his mariners to him and instructed him to "climb up into the Crow's Nest and call out **when you see <u>anything different!</u>**" The veteran captain knew that they were so far away from land that if they saw anything besides the ocean water, the sky and what was on the ships it had to come from land! So, he further theorized that if the seaman saw a bird, a piece of driftwood or anything different—land is nearby! It would not matter if they could see the land—if anything out of the ordinary was seen—**land is not far off!**

Similarly, when you obey God—know that the act of obedience galvanizes God into action! ***Look for a change!*** For God is at work and/or the Devil is busy! Whenever God is at work, Satan is busy seeking to counter the move of God! But make no mistake about it God and Satan are always busy in our lives! God's business is to accomplish Divine Agenda through our lives and Satan's mission is to thwart, frustrate and hinder God's program! Then, there are the times when Satan is the antagonist and God counteracts demonic intent.

So, whether the change that comes is Righteous and Holy by nature or diabolical and devilish—be heartened and cheered because it means that both principal participants in the drama of our lives have taken notice and are playing their parts! And, Children of Faith, I've read the last chapter and WE WIN! Celebrate that there is a change and rejoice and honor the change even when the change seems to be the harbinger and forerunner of a worse condition!

Never forget that Satan is the consummate liar; indeed he is the father of lies, an illusionist, a faker and he cannot do the truth! ***When he speaketh a lie, he speaketh of his own: for he is a liar, and the father of it.*** (John 8:44)

The beauty of Ezekiel's act of obedience was that while he prophesied—Ezekiel saw the change! He witnessed the results of his obedience! He saw "a shaking!" He heard "a shaking!" The clacking of bone against bone as they came together must have been a great noise for the bones were the remnant of a great army!

He saw and heard the bones finding their partner! Bones had fallen in a certain place when the soldiers were killed but had been blown by winds or washed away by torrential rains to a place some distance from the place where they had rested for untold years, Ezekiel now saw them being pushed and nudged by an unseen Hand! He witnessed them roll or levitate above the ground back to the place where the rest of their skeletal form was joining bone to bone! Then, perhaps he must have thought that his eyes were deceiving him because he saw some bones appear out of nowhere. These were bones that had been eaten by scavenging wolves, bears etc. They had to be recreated! They had to reappear!

It is likely that all of the bones were not as they had lain when the body fell! Some may have been half eaten or completely eaten by wild animals while some may have been covered up by the blowing of the wind and moved about by the rains. But they were all brought back in one cacophony of sound! Imagine Ezekiel's joy at the demonstration of the raw Power of God up close and personal! It was because Ezekiel spoke God's Word at God's command that out of chaos—order came and harmony as each one found its mate; bone to his bone!

Now imagine the joy of the Lord that will evoke such praises as we have never given God before if the Saints will just obey God, trust God, rely on His Word and anticipate His promises coming to pass in our lives!

A Feather from the Eagle's Wings

*"You know your trust in God is real and pure when the answers are **no longer necessary!**"*

CHAPTER 46

———⇒•0•⇐———

DEAD TO LIVE

Eze 37:8 And when I beheld, lo, the sinews and the flesh came up upon them, and the skin covered them above: but *there was* no breath in them.

Ezekiel speaks from a heart that is filled with amazement when he records, **"and when I beheld, lo ..."** The word, "lo" is an expletive that is forced from the mouth of one who is awestruck, amazed and in great fascination in response to something that was beyond the ordinary and mundane and in complete contrast to and sometimes, violation of—the norm.

How did it happen! How did the sinews and the flesh "come up upon them?" Did the skin seem to appear out of nowhere to cover them? Did the skin just appear on the bones?

"... but *there was* no breath in them."

What a big build up for a big let down! All dressed up with no ability to go! These are some of the responses that may come from the mouths of those who are too satisfied too quickly!

Not to worry though because the Father and Creator of all the Earth never leaves a job unfinished! It will not give Him maximum glory to simply "dress up" the bones in His finest sinew, flesh and skin. Such an array of bodies could not praise and worship God! They could not fight for Him! At that time and in that condition they had the very best that they could have without the breath of life in them! The very best they had was POTENTIAL! However, they did not have potential because of their great number or by reason of their weapons that were still scattered about the valley floor. No! They had great potential because **God had a Plan!** *Divine Will and Purpose had need of them!*

Suffice it to say, "Lying on the ground was *potentially a great army!*" But in that condition, they were only a viable force **"in potential"** for they had no life in them! How very much like some church folk these bodies were! They had the appearance of life but not the energy of life. They had the promise of doing but had no fulfillment. As the saying goes, *"All dressed up with nowhere to go!"* If the Body of Christ would develop the proper intimacy with God He would reveal to them that if they will remain faithful to Him He will ensure their arrival at their destiny! **God, Himself, will see to it that they reach their potential!** In truth, Jesus promised, **"Verily, verily, I say unto you, He that believeth on me, the works that I do shall he do also; and greater works than these shall he do; because I go unto my Father."** (John 14:12 KJV) Jesus further promised, **"They shall take up serpents; and if they drink any deadly thing, it shall not hurt them; they shall lay hands on the sick, and they shall recover."** (Mar 16:18) **What potential the Children of God have!**

CHAPTER 47

PREACHING: THE BREATH OF LIFE

"Then said he unto me, Prophesy unto the wind, prophesy, son of man, and say to the wind, Thus saith the Lord GOD; Come from the four winds, O breath, and breathe upon these slain, that they may live." (Eze 37:9)

"How then shall they call on him in whom they have not believed? and how shall they believe in him of whom they have not heard? and how shall they hear without a preacher? And how shall they preach, except they be sent?" (Rom 10:14-15(a) KJV)

It is a fact that God could have simply spoken His Infallible Word and the bones would have come alive! But it is of paramount importance to Him that His people become His children in terms of living His Likeness! Ezekiel never heard Jesus promise, **"Verily, verily, I say unto you, He that believeth on me, the works that I do shall he do also; and greater works than these shall** he do; because I go unto my Father." (John 14:12 KJV) God has always desired for his children to emulate Him!

Ezekiel was to prophesy unto the wind. Please understand what prophesying is. While preaching is *forth telling*—prophesying is *foretelling!* Preaching tells **what was** and **what is** while prophesying tells of **what shall be!** Ezekiel is to forth tell the winds to release the breath; the spirit of life upon these slain that they may live! Just as the Apostle, Paul, recorded that the Lord said, **"Oh death where is your sting"** and **"Oh grave, where is your victory?"** So, now is Ezekiel to announce the Will of God to the Breath of life saying, **"Come from the four winds, O breath, and breathe upon these slain, that they may live."**

The Savior reasons with the church in Rom. 10:14-15 saying, **"How then shall they call on him in whom they have not believed? and how shall they believe in him of whom they have not heard? and how shall they hear without a preacher? And how shall they preach, except they be sent?** The same principles apply in Ezekiel's life regarding the winds and the bones. The winds could not release the Breath of Life and the Breath of Life could not make the bones live **if no preacher had called; if no preacher had been sent** and **if no one had prophesied!**

"Oh, Breath of Life if you don't breathe upon these bones they will never realize their potential; destinies will never be reached and faith will forever be thwarted in these lives!"

251

Calls are still being sent out to all who will heed the battle cry and take up arms against death and corruption! *The dead can live again; the corrupt can be saved and the dying can be healed* **if someone would cry out to them;** *if* **someone would preach to them.** *If Someone would prophesy to them!*

A Feather from the Eagle's Wings

"God cannot change because he already is what he could become!"

CHAPTER 48

---◆---

HALLELUJAH-TOSIS: THE BREATH OF A SECOND CHANCE

Herein Is The Key To The True Value Of A Second Chance

Eze 37:10 So I prophesied as he commanded me, and the breath came into them, and they lived, and stood up upon their feet, an exceeding great army.

Ezekiel was true to his calling. He prophesied just as God ordered him to. And lo! The breath of life came into them. And they lived! They breathed because the prophet prophesied *the Breath of a second chance!* But they could not dream—yet. They could not aspire—yet! They could not praise and worship the God of their second chance! They had a second chance know and love the Lord and they stood up an exceeding great army! They had life but had no living!

How very much like so many in the church today this army was. Making up an exceeding great army having life but seeming to have no power, purpose or destiny! But, just as the All Wise God had not finished with this army so is He not finished with His Church!

When the breath of life came into them they were not only empowered to live—they were destined to fight! Otherwise they would have been a very large crowd not "an exceeding great army!" This should galvanize into action all who name the name of Christ for the sake of the Kingdom! Because there are yet those who in times past walked among us but are now dead in their trespasses and sins who need raising from that lowly estate to again" **sit together in heavenly places in Christ Jesus.**" (Eph 2:6 KJV) There is also the number who sleepwalks; unmindful of the terrible eternity that awaits them. There are still the fallen who "can't get up!" And there are still the disillusioned who need inspiration! And let us not forget those who are suffering from the bludgeoning of their own consciences remembering misdeeds done that they think cannot be undone!

Prophesy, Saints of God! Command fresh breath to give new strength! Command fresh fire to create new inspiration!

A Feather from the Eagle's Wings

Without who you were—you could not be who you are. Omit any major event in your life and you could not be who you came to be!

CHAPTER 49

WHAT THEY KNOW IS WHAT THEY "SAY" AND WHAT THEY "SAY" IS WHAT THEY GET!

Eze 37:11 Then he said unto me, Son of man, these bones are the whole house of Israel: behold, they say, Our bones are dried, and our hope is lost: we are cut off for our parts.

No doubt, Ezekiel was in great wonder as to who this army was. They were, as the Lord of Hosts said, *"the whole house of Israel."* Jehovah, God, then began to rehearse to Ezekiel, Israel's opinions concerning their past; their present and their future.

What Israel knows is what they say and what they say is what they get! They know that their bones are dead! They know that their bones are dried up! They know that their bones are so dead that there is no hope for their future! And they are **"... snared with the words of ... their mouth." (Prov. 6:2)** According to Proverbs 23:7 "... **as he**

257

thinketh is his heart so is he." I have very often observed that" Our **thoughts** will become our actions; our actions will become our habits and our habits will become our character!" In the instance of the dry bones of this valley as well as of Israel, the *"knowing"* produced a mindset that caused and action! It is recorded that *based on what they know*—"they say!"

"They say," in this instance, is a most powerful observation. For what *"they* say" about themselves has everything to do with what *they* achieve and what they don't achieve! What *"they* say" will determine who and what they are to themselves. Who and w*hat they are to themselves* will decide their presentation to the world. Tragically, what *"they say"* will determine what they even expect of their God! For, what *they* don't see as a real possibility for themselves—*they* **won't ask God for! Remember, "Ye have not because ye ask not."** (Jas. 4:2b)

"Our bones are dried up! Our infrastructure; that which our sinews, muscles and ligaments should be attached to *are dried up*! We have had our day! We have used up all of our opportunities and chances! Our day is past and our night has come!" They didn't live long enough to hear Jesus say it but they most certainly would have agreed with Him when He said, ". . . **the night cometh when no man can work!"** (John 9:4)

It is bad enough that our bones are dried up but they are as well severed and separated from one another. They are not part of a whole. God's children complained, ". . . **we are cut off for our parts."** Our parts have no agreement or fellowship with one another. They are not able to have a purpose. For, what can be done with parts that are not joined to anything? And no part that is missing (feels the loss of) its other parts!

Without leadership; without singleness of mind and having no purpose—the bones (God's scattered people)" could not help themselves! The plight of Israel was indeed grim! Such is the plight of all who allow themselves to be separated from the heart and the mind of their creator!

CHAPTER 50

---◆◇◆---

THE GREAT "GRAVEBREAK"

Eze 37:12 Therefore prophesy and say unto them, Thus saith the Lord GOD; Behold, O my people, I will open your graves, and cause you to come up out of your graves, and bring you into the land of Israel.

I promise you I will open your graves and cause you to come up out of your graves," God proclaimed. *They don't <u>know</u> this* so God must tell them! Their grave is all too real! Their bondage had been for a seeming eternity. The time is past for delusions of grandeur and lofty ideas of dreams fulfilled. For their bones are, after all, **dried up!**

So, God shouts His promise not only to those whose bones were dried but to their futures as well, **"I WILL OPEN YOUR GRAVES; I WILL CAUSE YOU TO COME UP OUT OF YOUR GRAVES, AND BRING YOU INTO THE LAND OF ISRAEL!"** If they never know the promise *they will never look for its fruition!* They will never hold out for the miracle! The promises of God are their leverage and anchor! Only the promise that they

Know will multiply their stamina and their durability! It will keep them from panicking! It will provide the staying power and see them through the drought of life and the famine of hope and sustain them until the time of the latter rain that is surely to come! **But they must know the promise!** They must expect the truth (the promise of God) to live *in their lifetime*! It is small wonder that the Loving Lord instructed His children to **"Believe in the Lord your God, so shall ye be established; believe his prophets, so shall ye prosper. (2nd Chron.20:20)** No one can believe having no knowledge of what to believe or who to believe! How on point the Apostle, Paul was when He questioned, ". . . **and how shall they believe in him of whom they have not heard?"** (Rom 10:14)

   "Behold, O My people," God is saying. *"Listen to me, My children, My dry bones!"* I am not through with you yet! I have made you! I have given you life! I have put My spirit in you! I have prepared you for freedom and victory!"

   "But," He is still saying to us today, *"You are still bound! You are still too close to the way things use to be! You are still feeling the pull and the constraints of your days of slavery to self and to Sin! You are still molded to your former ways!"*

   God is ever following the Love of His Eternal Heart! *"Oh My people, I must bring you out of your graves! I must free you from that place you call "home" and that way that you call your "life." I know that you have been locked in the grave of your flesh; your ways; your life for so long that it's hard for you to see yourself in any other place. But try to see through My eyes! Feel with My Heart the joy of the life that I have planned for you to live! Trust Me! Only trust Me! Purely trust Me!"*

"I will free you!" He is saying to His body of believers, *"I __must__ free you for if I don't open your graves you will stay there—all dressed up with nowhere to go! If I don't open your graves My plan will be forever frustrated! I must open your graves because you cannot do it for yourselves; no one else can! So, __I will__ __open your graves!__"*

He further explains, *"You will not open your graves because they are __"your graves!"__ They are yours! You know them! They define who you are to yourselves and to others! They are not only your graves—they are your bondage; they are your dungeons; they are your prisons! They have been your identity and you fight to keep them because you believe they are all you have! They are not only yours—__they are YOU!__ You don't know how to say, "That is where I have lived but that is not who I am! You never say, "that is what I did but that is not who I am! However, now I am here,"* the heart of God is saying, *"and I am here to open your graves and cause you to come up out of your graves and take you into the land of Israel; __take you home!__"*

"There will be a new order now because I""...**will cause you to come up out of your graves, and bring you into the land of Israel."** Can you hear the Love of God explain, *"If leave you to your own devices you will play it safe! You will opt for the familiar; the traditional! But because I love you with an everlasting love I will cause you to come up out of your graves and enter into a land of my choosing; a world of a new tomorrow with new possibilities; a world that is*

tailor made for you. In my world the trials will never be greater than you can bear. The victory will always be sweet and the joy will ever overflow! There is "the land of Israel." *"There is the "Secret Place of the Most High!" "There is a place you will call home!"* He reminds His people, *"There still is the Shadow of the Almighty where you will say, 'The Lord is my refuge and my fortress . . .'" "In this land of His Eternal Peace (His Eternal Presence) you will declare to all, He is ". . . my God, in Him will I trust."* (Psm. 91:2)

A Feather from the Eagle's Wings

When you know that you are spiritually weak—make NO major decisions!

CHAPTER 51

―――⟫⟩◦⟨⟪―――

THE GREAT GREAT GRAVEBREAK

Matt. 27:50 **"Jesus, when he had cried again with a loud voice, yielded up the ghost. And behold, the veil of the temple was rent in twain from the top to the bottom and the earth did quake, and the rocks rent. And the graves were opened; and many bodies of the saints which slept arose," Matt. 27:52) "And came out of the graves after his resurrection, and went into the holy city, and appeared unto many."**

Precious Heart, you must know that nothing ever shook up Creation more than **"The Great Gravebreak!"** For this was the second stage in the four steps of God's plan for the Redemption of Man.

1. The Virgin Birth
2. Death, burial of the Jesus Christ
3. Resurrection of Christ
4. The Rapture of the Church

Those who know these truths will live on a plane far and above those who are merely Christians who know about God and don't know God, His Word and His Promises

"Jesus . . . cried out <u>with a loud voice</u> . . . !" He made sure that everyone knew that He was not whipped. He was not defeated! He was still strong; still vibrant; yet a Force to be reckoned with! He **"cried out with a loud voice"** until Death knew that He was coming for the keys! He cried out loudly enough for Hell to know to get ready to handover its keys! Jesus cried with a loud voice until the grave knew that it was just a matter of time before the keys of death would be required and of this demand—the Son of God would not be denied!

Be reminded of the incident in Jesus' life when He raised Lazarus from the dead. Again, **"And when he thus had spoken, <u>he cried with a loud voice,</u> Lazarus, come forth." (John 11:43)** This He did ". . . **for the glory of God, that the Son of God might be glorified thereby." (John 11:4)**

Remember, **Jesus ". . . yielded up the ghost . . . ."**(Matt. 27:50) The word, **"yielded"** connotes that he *"laid aside, put or sent away; yielded up"* His Life's Spirit." (Strong's exhaustive Concordance #NT:863) In John 10:18, Jesus said, *"No man taketh it . . . (My life) . . . from me, but I lay it down of myself. I have power to lay it down, and I have power to take it again."* If he had not yielded up the Ghost He could never have died because there was no power great enough take His life and no mind genius enough to thwart God's Will! Further, there was no will strong enough to change the Father's Mind!

CHAPTER 52

DEAD AND REFUSING TO DIE!

"No man taketh it ... (My life) ... from me, but I lay it down of myself. I have power to lay it down, and I have power to take it again." (John 10:18)

This act of self-sacrifice is amazing enough but when you realize that in order for Jesus to *"lay down"* His life or *"put"* or *"send"* His life away, <u>He had to be able to outlive His death!</u> In human life no man has any influence on the world or the inhabitants of the world after His death unless he made a will. And then his will has no more strength than the integrity of the executor who enforces the will! The deceased cannot speak from the grave nor in anyway affect the world he left!

It is one thing for the believer to pray for the dead and believe for the miracle of a reawakening and another thing altogether for the deceased to, from the world of the dead—have control over anything!

But it was the **Word** ... that ... **was God** (John 1:1) **Who** declared in Jer. 1:12, **"I will <u>hasten</u> my word to**

perform it." According to Biblesoft's New Exhaustive Strong's Numbers and Concordance with Expanded Greek-Hebrew Dictionary, *"hasten"* is translated from a Hebrew word; entry # OT:8245, the word, *"shaqad (shaw-kad')* and means *"to be alert, i.e. sleepless; hence to be on the lookout."* Do you see it through the Spirit, Child of the King? Has it registered in your heart? For Jesus to "Give up the ghost"—*He had to outlive His death!* He had to (on some plane) stay alive to "be alert and remain "sleepless" so that he could "be on the lookout" to "perform" his Word! For, once He lost consciousness He could not "hasten His Word to perform it!"

So, *The Knowing* quite naturally floods the heart that—He was more than just a man! He had to be more than just Mary's boy! The *"knowing"* screams out to be revealed, understood, accepted and manifested! The *"knowing* is the Truth that declares, **"Jesus is not only Man! Jesus is God!"** How can one not know this truth in the face of such overwhelming evidence? Once this truth is revealed to you; once you *know* this truth—the possibilities become unlimited; the realities are more than earth can afford and all that Heaven offers! If Jesus was more than a man—I can believe to do the greater works; I can finally walk as a son of God among men! For I KNOW that if I KNOW I am a son of God than (concerning my spirit man) **I am a god** and "... **can do all things through Christ which strengthens me!"** I can "... speak of things that are not as though were" and watch the miraculous occur! Then when **"the earnest expectation of the creature waiteth for the manifestation of the sons of God,"** the lost soul will find in me a trueborn son of the living God with all of the powers and authorities of my Father at the ready!

A Feather from the Eagle's Wings

One of the greatest measures of God's Power is realized when you reach beyond the "break!"

CHAPTER 53

THE VALUE OF A TORN VEIL

"Keys to Appreciating the Value of the "Rent Veil are in this Chapter!"

"The practice of separating the believer from the Savior was abolished forever!"

Picture it! You have a need that only the Power, Wisdom and Love of the Almighty God can satisfy! Your physical health is failing; the condition is terminal! Perhaps you face a judge and jury for a crime you know you committed and the case is open and shut! All the evidence points to you as the guilty party! Or your teenage son is determined to self-destruct! Drugs, alcohol, sex and just plain rebellion and contempt for all things lawful and decent are what he lives for! Maybe your thirteen years old daughter has been raped by a man who has given the AIDS virus to her and her unborn child that he planted in her! You would surely want to help them; to save them from what they are doing and from what has been done to them! You have taken them to family counseling. You have gotten each of them specialized therapy. You have moved the family numerous times to give everyone a chance for a brand new start! And, to make them know how special they are, you have bought them things they said they wanted. You have also denied them things they shouldn't have! Because you love them so much!

Then, what if you know your family is violent? You don't want them to hurt anybody else or to endure further injury to themselves. And what do you do if you can't go to God because you have no access to Him! You know that you have gone to priests and asked for prayer for your family. You even paid to have sacrifices made to God so that he might intervene on behalf of your family.

But nothing worked! You see nothing but a dismal life of failure and shame in their future! You *know* that if you could just go to God for yourself *you could touch His heart*! You just don't feel that anybody cares *like you care* and you are convinced that the way people pray is based on how their heart feels about an issue! So, you can see no way out but to shoot them all to death while they sleep! That is the only method you can come up with to save them from themselves and others from them!

"The veil of the Temple was rent ...."

The veil separated the Holy Place from the Most Holy Place. All priests could go into the Holy Place but only the High Priest could go into the Holiest of Holies or the Most Holy Place and then only once a year. Now, for the first time in the history of the world, every man has access to the Holiest of Holies; everyone has the right of

271

entrance into the very Presence of God! For, now, in the New Testament Church, the Lord invites **us to "... come boldly unto the throne of grace."** *(Heb.4:16)*

If man had torn the veil it would have probably been torn from the bottom to the top. But man did not tear the veil! When the veil was torn from the top to the bottom Heaven responded to the death of the Son of God! Heaven announced to all the earth that the middle wall of petition between God and man, symbolized by the veil that separated the Holiest of Holies from the Holy Place, was destroyed! The practice of separating the believer from the Savior was abolished forever!

Equally important is the fact that the veil represented the body (flesh) of Jesus. That the veil was rent (torn) is a fitting illustration of the suffering; the torture that the Body of Christ endured. To rend something is not to merely cut it as with a pair of scissors or neatly and cleanly as with a knife! To rend is to tear with no purpose in mind but to destroy quickly; to cause terrible damage immediately! A fitting description of rending is clearly seen in the ferocious attack of a lion on a deer! The lion usually does not hunt unless it is hungry. So when it kills its prey it is not likely to eat daintily, observing good manners! It usually tears right in to the meal with the emphasis on the word, "tear" or to follow the text of the lesson, **"rend!"** "Destruction" is the optimum word here! Remember, Dear one, **"the temple was rent!**

In rending, the goal may or may not be death! There is not the slightest measure of concern for the aesthetics; beauty or even of professionalism in the act! And that was exactly the purpose of the crucifixion—**to rend!** The only and the major difference between just rending and the crucifixion is that the ultimate goal was death!

It is interesting that the artwork and sculpture that you find in some churches and in many pictures that are to depict the crucifixion of Jesus is terribly devoid of real signs and indications of the bloody mess that Jesus was! The pictures show a couple of neat little trickles of blood here and there but nothing to offend the delicate senses.

But, as the prophet, Isaiah put it, "...**he hath no form nor comeliness; and when we shall see him,** *there is* **no beauty that we should desire him. (Isa. 55:2)**

Indeed, **"He is brought as a lamb to the slaughter."** **(Isa. 53:7)**

Can you imagine what the carcass of a slaughtered lamb looks like? Those who slaughter animals don't treat them with deference, respect or reverence! Jesus was beaten, bludgeoned, clubbed, whipped and tortured!

They even snatched his beard out from the roots! **"I gave my back to the smiters, and my cheeks to them that plucked off the hair: I hid not my face from shame and spitting."** (Isa 50:6)

But suddenly, there is a new hope in the air; a new day has dawned and tomorrow has a great future! The veil is rent! We who couldn't even see into the Holiest of Holies now can not only see into it—we can actually cross the threshold and enter it! The benefits of the Tabernacle, the Church and the Body of Christ are not hidden from us anymore! We don't have to try to gain access into the Presence of God by dead works or by sacrificing things! There is no separating veil! All who know and have faith in this miraculous truth will call it, "Precious!"

Perhaps the reason these artists have an almost bloodless sacrifice at Calvary is that they are too squeamish to face the reality of the Crucifixion. Man often will lie to himself in order to not have to face certain realities. Interesting isn't it that they want their sins covered with the Blood of Jesus but they don't want to be reminded of the Shed Blood!'

Not only did the torture mess Him up but (2Co 5:21) ". . . he hath made him *to be* sin for us, who knew no sin." Ever wondered what a person would look like who literally became the sin of the world? ". . . **he hath no form nor comeliness; and when we shall see him,** *there is* **no beauty that we should desire him** . . . ." I have seen people who have been so terribly burned that the scar tissue was layered on top of layer. To say that they were grotesque and even monstrous in their appearance is to put it mildly. Jesus, however, was so misshapen (spiritually) that He had no definable shape. He was not round, square, elongated, triangular or rectangular. He had no form! The mass of sin was shapeless and ugly! There was no beauty that any should desire Him!

"The earth did quake!" In 1836 Ralph Waldo Emerson wrote of the *"**Shot** heard 'round the world"* in his "Concord Hymn" that memorialized the men that gave their lives at the first battle of the <u>American Revolution</u>. However, when Jesus died, the earthquake that followed was "the *shock* heard and felt round the world." On top of the earth, the message was received that in preparation for the inauguration of the dispensation of Grace, there was a new order and regime in the earth.

When Jesus "yielded up the ghost" all of the sins that had ever been committed since Adam sinned in the Garden of Eden; that great mass of sin that Jesus became—*entered into the earth at one time!* And that much sin was just too much for the earth's constitution! Could it be that the earth just couldn't take it and gave itself to its throes of vomiting, churning and roiling! The earth bucked and threw itself in vain efforts to accept what it could not accept and *what it could not deny!* The Body that Life had lived in was being interred in the earth!

The earth had opened its great maw and swallowed sinful souls since the first death in Eden. But even then, the voice of a brother's blood was heard crying out from the ground! (Gen 4:10) But when Jesus yielded up the ghost it is almost as if, on some level of spiritual plane, "Hope" and "Resurrection" were in the earth straining to finally win the battle against the finality of death and the grave! It's as if Hope and Resurrection fought to win for all of those souls that died in the faith **"not accepting deliverance." (Heb. 11:5)** It is as if they knew and anticipated that the Apostle, Paul, would one day shout that clarion call of triumph, **"O death, where *is* thy sting? O grave, where *is* thy victory?"** (1Co15:55) The time was not yet—though a few souls had been brought back to life after succumbing to the relentless clutches of death and the grave.

The rocks rent!" Boulders that took thousands of years to be formed and have withstood untold pressures of storms of wind, rain, snow and sleet and even the hottest heat that the Lord would send "RENT! They were broken apart! They were smashed by the powerful force of earth's new reality! The final and fatal blow had been dealt to the deepest echelons of Satan's diabolical plan and purpose! Satan is now on notice as never before that the price for the ultimate end of his reign of terror over the earth *is paid!* The whole world felt the aftershocks both of the Son of God leaving this world and His entering the portals of the grave! Earth would never be the same again! This momentous event was worthy of the most glorious fanfare played by the greatest trumpeters and the most proficient percussionists of all time! There should have been a pyrotechnic show of fireworks that would rival the exploding of a nova; the brilliance of colliding suns and the Northern lights, the "Auro ra Borealis," all at one glorious time! But that was what man might have imagined as an offering to herald the news of the death of the Son of God!

Heaven's "Great Event Planner" orchestrated a cacophony of both movement and sound; the tangible and the intangible coming together in a fusion and a blend of the wondrous and macabre; the magnificent and the gruesome! Consider change of events and the response in the earth:

1. **Jesus, when he had <u>cried</u>** (Noise)
2. <u>**again with a loud voice,**</u> (More Nois*e*)
3. **yielded up the ghost.** (Earth Robbed of a Life)
4. **And behold, the veil of the temple was rent in twain from the top to the bottom** (Divine Vandalism)

5. **and the earth did quake,** (Instability of our Foundation)
6. **and the rocks rent.** (Cemetery Security Breached)
7. **And the graves were opened;** (First stanza of "Free at Last")
8. **and <u>many bodies of the saints</u> which slept <u>arose</u>," Matt. 27:52)** ("Great Waking up Morning")
9. **"And came out of the graves after his resurrection, and (**Great Grave Break)
10. **went into the holy city, and** (Redefining of Hope)
11. **appeared unto many."** (Now all may celebrate the Hope of the Church!)

"The graves were opened "Even the underworld (the grave) gave way to the power of the new order! It is noteworthy at this point to mention that in every other instance of this experience the earth simply had a reaction (seemingly of a natural cause) to the death of the Christ. That is to say, **"The earth *did quake and the rocks rent!*"** But God very directly and with purpose inspired Matthew to record, **"The *<u>graves were opened</u>*!"** The graves did not open because of the earthquake—THEY **_WERE OPENED!_** The graves did not open because of happenstance or inadvertence but as a result of divine intervention. **". . . And many bodies of the saints which slept arose," Matt. 27:52)** All of the graves didn't open! Not even all of the bodies of the saints arose. Rather, **"<u>Many bodies of the saints that slept arose</u> . . . ."** Remember, Dear Heart, despite what death is to the sinner, it is only sleep to the saints of God and *the grave is merely where our bodies sleep!* It was a matter most small for the Life of life to give life to (or wake) those who were only sleep!

Feather's from the Eagle's Wings

The Old man sees earth's possibilities while the New man sees Heaven's realities as possibilities.

CHAPTER 54

YOU MUST *KNOW* WHO
AND *WHAT* YOU ARE

A Key element that is needed to fulfill
your destiny is found in this chapter.

*"In order to fulfill your destiny—you must know who
and what you are!"*

In order to fulfill your destiny—you must know who and what you are! Many Church people remain all too close to who they were before they were born again. Many have a false sense of their own worth. In their humility and their desire to make it known that they see God as the Almighty they lower themselves down into false humility and that is not the desire of their Father! While they are bowing and scraping before the Father—He desires them to take their rightful places in this world as "sons of God!" **Beloved, NOW are we the sons of God." (1ˢᵗ John 3:2)**

Note that no reasonable person would doubt or contest that the son of a lion is a lion or that the son of an alligator is an alligator. All expect the son of a horse to be a horse. But the erroneous expectation that men have for God is for Him to have something other than a god for His sons. When the Jews sought to stone Him for calling Himself God, **"Jesus answered them, Is it not written in your law, I said, Ye are gods?" Joh 10:35 "If he called them gods, unto whom the word of God came, and the scripture cannot be broken . . . ! (Joh 10:34)** In proving His that He is God—Jesus mentions a truth that they all accepted as from God—their own law! Jesus includes even the Jews as being gods. His reasoning is 1) your own law (scriptures) announces that you are gods and 2) if He (God) called them gods to whom the word of God had to come then *ye <u>are gods</u>* because the scripture cannot be broken! The scripture cannot be "dissolved, destroyed, melted or broken" according to Strong's #G3089)!

"The scripture cannot be broken!"Thus the reasoning says to all, If He called *you* gods—then <u>you must conclude, *I am surely a god!*</u> The point of this line of thinking is—it is high time for the Saints of the Most High to learn and to live the truth of what they are! **If the son of a lion is a lion**—then the son of the Lion of Judah—IS A LION! It is time for the sons of The Lion to stand up in all of the power and might that their Father will give them to wield! It is time for The Lion's sons to roar with His voice and fight with His prowess and WIN victories IN HIS NAME!

Feathers from the Eagle's Wings

None can walk with confidence who don't know that they belong where they are!

CHAPTER 55

FAITH IS ABOUT GIVING
GOD A NAME

A Key to Knowing What to Name
your God is in this Chapter!

*"If the name the **you give God** is limited to what
earth has to offer **let not the giver of the name expect
anything from Heaven!"***

What is in a name? What is the power of a name! What
makes "a good name . . ." **"rather to be chosen than great
riches?"** (Pro. 22:1)

The most powerful thing that any love can give is
the name of the lover whether is through the bonds of
marriage or through the instrument of Power of Attorney!
Indeed, in a marriage, the name can outlive the name giver.
When a man gives to his bride his name, he has given
her access to everything that he possesses unless particular
laws prevent it!

Along with some names come certain authorities, expectations, understandings, privileges, honors and dishonors. The person who is held in great and high esteem will provide to those whose privilege it is to use his name—entrances and accessibilities and position and benefits that those who only know the most revered one *casually* can never attain to.

All that the believer and the non-believer expect of Jesus has to do with the name that each of them has assigned to the Lord. And **neither has the right** to **expect or demand anything but what the assigned name can afford him!** If the name that you give God *is limited to what earth has to offer* **let not the giver of the name expect anything from Heaven!** If the name that is given to our Lord is Holy and Righteous then the giver of the name will never ask for what hell approves!

"A good name . . ." being **"rather to be chosen than great riches,"** (Pro. 22:1) has nothing to do with the popularity of a name, the number of syllables, or letters that make a word but in this passage of scripture has reference to one's character. If one's character is unimpeachable and above reproach, then it is that the expectations, the understandings and privileges that honorable people will have and will offer to the person in question will be of the highest order. If the character of the individual who is at issue is shady, unreliable or in any way unsavory and objectionable then the individual (the character) will be seen in a bad light and success will elude him!

In speaking of a time in the disciples near future, Jesus promised, "... **in that day ye shall ask me nothing. Verily,**

verily, I say unto you, Whatsoever ye shall ask the Father <u>in my name</u>, he will give *it* you. (Joh 16:23) The day that Jesus spoke of is the day of his departure into His eternal destiny! He was heading for the Cross of Calvary! He would not be here to take their requests and respond to their needs but He did not leave them helpless or hopeless! He gave them the Power of Attorney! But their use was not unlimited authority! They could use His name but *only <u>in his name (His character)</u>!* Using His name *in His name* means that they could only use His name in the manner and only for the purposes that He would sanction; that He would approve; in ways that He would use His authority!

Joh 16:24 **Hitherto have ye asked nothing in my name: ask, and ye shall receive, that your joy may be full.**

Nothing was asked in the name of Jesus up to that time because He had not gone to the Cross yet and He had not the "Power of Attorney" to give. Jesus would fulfill His promise to His disciples to **". . . give unto . . . them ". . .the keys of the kingdom of heaven."** Further promising them, **"And whatsoever thou shalt bind on earth shall be bound in heaven and whatsoever thou shalt loose on earth shall be loosed in heaven."** But this would be after He rose from the grave and has **". . . the keys of hell and of death."** (Rev 1:18) (Mat 16:19) Actually He would give the Power of Attorney to His Children **"When he ascended up on high, he led captivity captive, and gave gifts unto men.** (Eph 4:8). That was the beginning-of-the-end of Satan's rule over man (at least *for the <u>people who Know</u>*)! Remember, **"It's all About The Knowing!"**

CHAPTER 56

IT'S STILL ALL IN *THE KNOWING!*

The Keys to Giving God What He wants is Learned in this Chapter!

*"**Knowing**" is the key to both pleasing God and to displeasing Him!"*

Whether the issue is spiritual or natural, everything we do is directed by, enhanced by, hindered by or in some way mitigated or positively influenced by *The Knowing* that leads or impedes us; drives or denies us!

The inescapable principles that are recurrent over and over in the scriptures prove that *"Knowing"* is the key to both pleasing God and to displeasing Him! From Eden throughout history it has been the presence or the absence of the *"Knowing"* that has caused the fingerprints of success or failure to make its mark in the lives of humanity! **One who intends to please God must simply give God what He wants**:

O nothing more

- ○ nothing less
- ○ and nothing else
- ○ no matter the cost!

In Eden, the serpent declared "... **in the day ye eat thereof ... ye shall know ...**! Even Jesus promised, **"Ye shall know ...!"** (John 8:32) The active ingredient in all things that our God approves is the empowering *"Knowing!"* **"But without faith *it is* impossible to please *him:* for he that cometh to God must believe that he is, and *that* he is a rewarder of them that diligently seek him."** (Heb11:6) No one can please God who does not know God because **pleasing God can never be the result of happenstance or inadvertence!** There is no accidental please God! Only by a purposeful and conscious act of faith that is founded on God's Righteousness can anything be done that will satisfy God or give Him something to delight in!

It is a fact that, usually, it is not the things *people know they are* that hinders them! Rather, it is the things *they know they are not* that hinders them! If you know that you are not a believer—you won't be a believer until you receive a *"Knowing"* that changes what you know! If you know that you are not a sower of spiritual seed you won't be a sower until you receive a *"Knowing"* that changes what you know!

There are those realities that have their origins in the earth realm and there are those that are Heaven based! Those earthly realities do not normally afford one the mindset to go against impossible odds with the intent to win! It is the Heavenly mind that sees what is not there and puts it there! The earthly mind will call "idiocy" and "stupidity" things that the **"Knowing"** mind *Knows* are the makings for a miracle!

Man needs the "Knowing" of God, which is a revelation of God! Man had the capacity to receive revelatory knowledge because as Elihu puts it in Job 32:8, **"But *there is* a spirit in man: and the inspiration of the Almighty giveth them understanding."** It is in the spirit that is in man that God wants to place inspiration and it is inspiration that provides the understanding! The Apostle, John writes, **"*That* was the true Light, which lighteth every man that cometh into the world.** (John 1I:9) That "Light" was the inspiration of the Almighty; the inspired Truth that gives them understanding; revelation and *Knowing*"!

A Feather from the Eagle's Wings

When you know that you are spiritually weak—DON'T MAKE ANY MAJOR DECISIONS!

CHAPTER 57

WHAT WE FOUGHT *WITH*, DENIED *FOR* AND STOOD *ON*

The Strategy Behind Your Winning Ways is in this Chapter!

"You won because" . . . *the weapons of* . . . *your* *". . . warfare . . ."* *were* *". . . not carnal, but mighty through God to the pulling down of strong holds."* (2Co 10:4)

"Cast not away therefore your confidence, which hath great recompense of reward." (Heb. 10:35)

It is ludicrous, absurd and altogether ridiculous that you would cast away the absolute conviction and certainty of victory that you used to fight Satan **with ! It makes no sense whatsoever that you would totally disparage and belittle the same convictions that you** denied yourself fleshly cravings *for* and stood *on* against virtually impossible odds!

Surely you cannot *at the point of triumph concede defeat* by throwing it all away!

Hence, now at the last you must not weaken nor falter! You *Know* too much! You have been through too much! You have, because of *The Knowing*, *become too much!* You must not <u>*now—while you approach the end*</u>—prove fickle and whimsical. You cannot allow ". . . **the trial of your faith** . . ." that the Father has deemed ". . . **much more precious than of gold that perisheth, though it be tried with fire** . . ." (meaning, pure gold) to be devaluated by human frailty and fleshly lusts! (See 1st Pet. 1:7)

- ❖ You fought using the weapons of your faith in

    - ○ the Word of God
    - ○ the Power of God
    - ○ the name of Jesus
    - ○ your love for God
    - ○ *the Knowing* of God's Love for you

- ❖ longsuffering and stamina,
- ❖ your devotion to His Son and the Body of Christ!

You also were bolstered and strengthened by your hope and expectation of victory in the battle. That and your confidence that the Rapture is soon to come kept you in the fight! Your hope, your expectation of victory and your confidence held you up at times when everything in you seemed to say. "It is over! I have lost! The enemy has won!" Yes, you fought sometimes with your head hung down; sometimes with shoulders that were slumped in virtual defeat! But you got back up and tried again! You fought again! And from the ashes of your life's destructions—**you rose!** You rose when every fiber of your being said, "Stay down! You will just become a target again if you stand!" But stand—you did! There was Something in you that was Indomitable! There was Someone in you Who would not be denied! You rose up in Him! You stood up in Him to fight again—and this time—TO WIN! And you won because "... **the weapons of** ... your" ... **warfare** ... were "... **not carnal, but mighty through God to the pulling down of strong holds** ...." (2Co 10:4) Though the enemy supposed and assumed that you were vulnerable, weak and exposed, he learned that you had on "... **the whole armour of God, that ye may be able to withstand in the evil day!**" And when Satan and your Old Man believed that you were defeated, finished and conquered, they learned that you were further armed with the mental and spiritual pre-determination that after you had "... **done all** ..., your mind was made up "... **to stand.**" (Eph 6:13)

Have you ever noticed the commonalities of character in those who were sold out to God regardless of the dispensation they lived in or their gender or calling? Have you noticed that they all seemed to be cut from the same spiritual and mental cloth? Their love and devotion to God compelled them to deny themselves, decline promotions and positions, turn down earthly treasures, refuse physical comforts and disagree with popular opinions.

Take Moses for example. He had not the indwelling of the Holy Spirit. But, see him, **"Choosing rather to suffer affliction with the people of God, than to enjoy the pleasures of sin for a season."**(Heb 11:25) **Esteeming the reproach of Christ greater riches than the treasures**

in Egypt: for he had respect unto the recompence of the reward. (Heb 11:26)

In addition, let's not forget "... **Stephen, a man full of faith and of the Holy Ghost,** (Act 6:5) It is further declared by the Apostle, Luke, that" ... **Stephen, full of faith and power, did great wonders and miracles among the people.** (Act 6:8) **But he, being full of the Holy Ghost, looked up stedfastly into heaven, and saw the glory of God, and Jesus standing on the right hand of God, And said, Behold, I see the heavens opened, and the Son of man standing on the right hand of God. Then they cried out with a loud voice, and stopped their ears, and ran upon him with one accord, And cast** *him* **out of the city, and stoned** *him:* **and the witnesses laid down their clothes at a young man's feet, whose name was Saul. And they stoned Stephen, calling upon** *God,* **and saying, Lord Jesus, receive my spirit. And he kneeled down, and cried with a loud voice, Lord, lay not this sin to their charge. And when he had said this, he fell asleep."** (Act 7:55-60)

What devotion to God! What resolve to be faithful no matter the cost! What an example of Godly strength and spiritual integrity! He was one whom Jesus spoke of in Rev. 12:11, **"And they overcame ... by the blood of the Lamb, and by the word of their testimony; and they <u>loved not their lives unto the death.</u>"**

What about you, O Gladiator for the Faith? When faced with your temptations in the flesh, you had a *Knowing* in your spirit that *your best was still to come*! You were more than willing to make the trade of earth's riches for Heaven's treasures. For, as the writer of the book of Hebrews puts it, *"ye . . . took joyfully the spoiling of your goods, <u>knowing</u> in yourselves that ye have in heaven a better and an enduring substance."* (Heb 10:34)

It truly is *"All in The Knowing!"* And that *"Knowing"* promises you that the joys of Heaven are real! They are not fictional figments of your imagination! Those joys are material substances that have real weight, value and promise! All that Earth has to offer in comparison to the realities of Glory are empty promises, futile gestures and shadows of things wished for. But the present hopes you have of Heaven are made of a substance that will endure throughout eternity; outliving time and running alongside "forever" for time without end! Even though you may never have articulated these truths, they were in the corridors of your heart, spurring and encouraging, hastening you and prompting you to pay whatever costs were assessed for your greatest hope and most magnificent and priceless dream; **the Rapture!**

Your *"Knowing"* made you believe that if you can just be a part of the Rapture of the Church and get *There, in Heaven,* where your treasures will never erode, corrode, rust or wear out—every sacrifice you made would have been vindicated. If you can just get *There* where thieves cannot break through and steal; where your foes cannot reach you or touch you—every trophy won from Satan and his hoards and your every testimony will be kept safe for all of eternity. Your *"Knowing"* gave you to believe with absolute certainty that if you can just get *There*—the scales will be more than balanced in your favor! All debts that were caused by your sufferings and your losses—will be settled! Every nightmare will be ended! Peace will prevail over frustration and all of your despairs, heartaches and soul breaks shall be swallowed up by Heaven's most exquisite joy! Yes, Precious Heart, I know just how you feel! For, my *Knowing* also tells me that if I can just get *"There"* everything will be perfect! In Heaven all will certainly be well!

Dear Christian, You must, at any cost, gain to yourself a *"Knowing"* that *within the Gates of that City called, "Heaven"* you shall have a life that is superior to this Earth realm in every way possible!

There you will know freedom—not because of broken shackles but because of the absence of the very concept of bondage! Rather than happiness, **you will experience a wonder of joy that this world cannot hope to offer.** For happiness is rather overrated being contingent on and subject to the desired *"happenings"* occurring! Heaven will be filled only with the things that are conducive to the most superb, most joyful joys God has to give! There, in Heaven, Saints of God, the reason you will have peace is not *because there is no war*—you will have peace because you will be in the raw Presence of the Prince of Peace and where He reigns—*there can be no hostilities; there can be no conflict!*

It is a fact that while Salvation is free—you will pay great and sometimes immeasurable costs to get to Heaven! This writer believes that the price you pay for something purchased is *the cost of the item* and the item itself *is the measure of the value you received.* So, you **must**, Saints of God, understand the reasoning of the learned Apostle, Paul, when he compares the costs of getting to Heaven with the untold joys of living there in the Eternal Presence of our Lord. Take a moment to contemplate 2nd Cor. 4:17-18 in the King James Version of the Bible. **"For our light affliction, which is but for a moment, worketh for us a far more exceeding *and* eternal weight of glory; While we look not at the things which are seen, but at the things which are not seen: for the things which are seen *are* temporal; but the things which are not seen *are* eternal.**

Now, please take note of the same passage in the Amplified Version. **For our light, momentary affliction (this slight distress of the passing hour) is ever more and more abundantly preparing and producing and achieving for us an everlasting weight of glory [beyond all measure, excessively surpassing all comparisons and all calculations, a vast and transcendent glory and blessedness never to cease!] 18 Since we consider and look not to the things that are seen but to the things that are unseen; for the things that are visible are temporal (brief and fleeting), but the things that are invisible are deathless and everlasting.**

It is very obvious by these considerations that, according to the Word of God, no matter the price we pay to get to Heaven—we have bought it in the bargain basement; we have purchased it cheaply!

It is imperative, Saints of the Most High God, that you stay before God until you receive from God a *"Knowing"* that will make Heaven so real, worthy and precious as to make the value of Heaven worth every price and worth that it may cost you.

Feathers from the Eagle's Wings

"One cannot succeed who does not have the courage to fail."

CHAPTER 58

———◆———

"His "Name" is More Than the word, "Jesus!" *Know* That!"

A Key To Answered Prayer and Pleasing God That Has Been Lost is Now Found!

". . . the name (the onoma) of Jesus when activated by faith—not the appellation or the word, "Jesus," <u>gets the job done!</u>"

It must be understood from the outset of this lesson that the word, "name" is not to be used (in this lesson) as a simple *appellation*. An *appellation* is a title or a label that differentiates between two or more things. If you are told to pick up a ball—you don't pick up the kite. The word "ball" is an appellation that *names* something that is vastly different from a kite. So, the word *"name,"* in this lesson, is descriptive of something more than an appellation; it is more than a label! For the purpose of this lesson the word *"name"* is the defining of the God-man, Christ Jesus. It is a defining of His purpose, His Power and His Love.

The Child of God faces a most formidable foe on a daily basis. Satan, man's nemesis and archenemy, has the advantage of having studied man since his encounter with man in the Garden of Eden. It is a fact that other than the Creator, Himself, nobody knows mankind as completely as does Satan! Satan and his demons interact with man daily. The trophies (reputations, opportunities, relationships, potentials and testimonies) that our adversary has taken from mankind since the genesis of all things are too numerous to mention.

Since man first sinned he has been in trouble with God and with his fellow man! He was too weak in his flesh to please God and was powerless to resist the devil! Without a doubt, there is not one human being *that has not felt and succumbed to the wiles of the devil—**but for the Man, Christ Jesus!***

I am reminded of one of my favorite Christmas carols, John Sullivan Dwight's version of "O Holy Night." Two of the phrases that always bless me are the ones that declare, *"Long lay the world in sin and error pining, 'til **He appeared** and the soul felt its worth."* Secondly, the songwriter explains, *"A thrill of hope; the weary world rejoices for yonder breaks a new and glorious morn!"* At the appearance of Jesus, the world was lifted and buoyed up with a hope it had never known before; that Satan would not forever conquer! Satan would not always win! The question, though, remained, "How would the Lord give humanity the victory? How was the fact of the Presence of the Lord to be used against the devil and his hoard of demons? The answer is—**His Name!**

The name of the Lord is the greatest, most multi-faceted, inexhaustible and invincible resource that believers have at their disposable! The **name** of the Lord is all about his feelings concerning His people and His willingness to come to the defense of His children.

As a weapon, the name of the Lord is both defensive and offensive. Observe that among other things, it is a place of refuge: "**The name of the Lord is a strong tower: the righteous runneth into it, and is safe.** Prov. (18:10) Towers were places that were built for both defense and offense. The "tower" was a safe place because it was usually built out of the reach of spear throwers and high enough that the arrows shot toward them may lose much of their effectiveness. But from the towers one could throw and shoot things down on the heads of their attackers.

"The righteous runneth into it and is safe!"

Though the righteous may not know this scripture, the righteous has spent enough time in the Presence of the Lord to know truths about the Lord that render the righteous—SAFE! According to *Biblesoft's New Exhaustive Strong's Numbers and Concordance with Expanded Greek-Hebrew Dictionary*, the transliteration of the word, "name" as it is used in proverbs 18:10 is, *OT#8034 "shem"—an appellation, as a mark or memorial of individuality; by implication honor, authority, character.)* Therefore, the word, *"name"* is more than an appellation; a word that distinguishes one thing from another. *"Shem"* is used as *"a mark or a memorial"* that reminds one of a heroic and honorable or cowardly and dishonorable person or deed. But, even more, *"shem"* implies the type of honor, type of authority and character and calling and purpose that one has on his/her life.

In the instance of this scripture, when the righteous are threatened, they immediately think of the best place to find refuge. The place of refuge must be easily accessible and within their rights to enter. It must as well be a proper defense that provides for a vigorous offense and one that will not bring them and their God dishonor. There is no better place for the righteous to find all that they desire for safety's sake than the Name of the Lord! For, it is because of *what God stands for* and because of *what He will not stand for* that He has the Name that He is known by.

The New Testament word, for *"name"* that is translated from the Greek language means the same as the word, *"shem"* that was used in the Old Testament. The New Testament word in the Greek language that is translated, "name" is the word, **"onoma"** (on'-om-ah); meaning a "name" (literally or figuratively) [authority, character] *Strong's NT #G3686*: When the word, *"onoma"* is used in reference to God, His authority and His Character, to include His Power, Nature and His Life's Purpose and Calling are brought to bear. The righteous may not know the word, **"name,"** as translated from the Hebrew or the Greek but they do know enough about the Spirit of God to expect that they may find refuge in His Authority, Character, Power and Nature and His Life's Calling.

In considering another aspect of the multi-faceted *"name* of the Lord,"* let us explore Acts 3:16. This episode in the life of Jesus deals with a paralyzed man who begged for alms as he sat at the gate called, "Beautiful." To cut to the chase, the man was healed! When an answer was sought as to why and how the man's healing occurred, the Apostle, Peter answered, **"And his _name_ through faith in his name hath made this man strong, whom ye see and know: yea, the faith which is by him hath given him this perfect soundness in the presence of you all."**

Pay strict attention to the fact that Peter did not say that *faith* made the man whole. Neither did he suggest that *the name of Jesus* healed this man. Rather, it was the Dynamic Duo working together. "... **his name ... (Onoma) ... through faith in his name ... (Onoma) ... hath made this man strong."** It takes faith to activate the name (Onoma—His Authority, Character, Power and Nature and His Life's purpose and calling!) Just invoking and appealing to the appellation, "Jesus" will never touch the Heart of God! (Remember the "sons of Sceva in Acts 19:113-16. **"Then certain of the vagabond Jews, exorcists, took upon them to call over them which had evil spirits the name of the Lord Jesus, saying, We adjure you by Jesus whom Paul preacheth. And there were seven sons of *one* Sceva, a Jew, *and* chief of the priests, which did so. And the evil spirit answered and said, Jesus I know, and Paul I know; but who are ye? And the man in whom the evil spirit was leaped on them, and overcame them, and prevailed against them, so that they fled out of that house naked and wounded."**

Now going back to Acts 3:16 and note that *the name (the onoma) of Jesus when activated by! It is not the appellation or the word, "Jesus," that gets the job done!* The **name** of Jesus **through faith in the name of** (the character etc.) of Jesus defeats Satan and rescinds satanic orders and decrees. Again, not **the name <u>as an appellation</u>** (a word that distinguishes one thing from another), rather, **His name *through faith in* His name** (His Onoma, meaning, His Authority, Character, Power and Nature and Life's purpose and calling) caused the man to be made whole!

So, when the righteous are in need, the righteous ***Knows*** and remembers the "**name** of the Lord;" meaning His Authority, His Character, His Power and his Nature and Life's purpose and calling. To ***Know*** His Authority is to know that all powers, forces, conditions, and circumstances, indeed all things, are subject to Him! To ***Know*** His Character is to believe in His Compassion, His Honesty and Integrity, His Trustworthiness and His agape Love! To Know His Nature is to realize that He cares and is devoted to you and cannot ignore you or be less than your" **. . . refuge and strength, a very present help in trouble. Psm (46:1)**

My friend, you know that in our societies we are known to have "given" names and surnames. And humankind is also prone to give "pet" names or "nick" names to those who are held in great affectation or in very low esteem. Harold may be called, "Harry" and Joseph may be known as "Joe" or "Joey." Those names are simply short versions of the given names. But then, we also rename people because of a trait or characteristic they have. Despite the fact that his name is Bartholomew, we may give him the "nick" name, "Slim" because of him being very skinny. And what about the guy who is so smart that he has earned the "nick" name, Einstein?"

Well, when we truly have ***the Knowing*** of the true purpose, authority and nature of Jesus we will clearly understand why His Name was called, "Jesus." We *Know* that the prophecy declared, **"And she shall bring forth a son, and thou shalt call <u>his name</u> JESUS: for he shall save his people from their sins,"** (Matt. 1:21) We must understand that it was not *the Son* that was being named here rather ***<u>the name that the Son would be called was being named!</u>*** Therefore, the name, "Jesus" was given to the Son because of His character traits and His calling! "... **He shall save his people from their sins.**" The appellation, "Jesus" is akin to the names Jehovah and Joshua which denotes the traits and characteristic of a Savior. In His role as Jehovah, a great part of God's mission was to save His chosen people. Joshua was also assigned the formidable task of saving the children of Israel from themselves and their enemies and leading them into the perfect will of God. Jesus means, "Savior." There was no other name that could be given Him when His **Onoma**—His Authority, Character, Power, Nature and Life's purpose and Calling was brought into focus and taken into consideration. ". . . **for he shall save his people from their sins,"** (Mat 1:21)

We call Him "Jesus" because that appellation does truly distinguish Him from all other deities, powers and authorities in this world; in the underworld and in the world of people's imaginations. Just know that **"God also hath highly exalted him, and <u>given him a name</u> . . .** (again the Greek word, "Onoma") . . . **which is above every (name . . . ."** (Yep, Onoma) (Php 2:10) **"That at the name . . .** (Onoma) . . . **of Jesus every knee should bow, of** *things* **in heaven, and** *things* **in earth, and** *things* **under the earth."** (Php 2:9) Call Him, **"Jesus,"** Saints, and He will answer the call with all of the resources of Heaven at hand! *Know* that!

EPILOGUE

For unto us was the gospel preached, as well as unto them: <u>but the word preached did not profit them, not being mixed with faith in them that heard it.</u> Heb 4:2 KJV

Finally, my Brothers and Sisters, if you have read and will reread these lessons in their entirety, and place these truths in your spirit, **The Knowing** (*God's Mind and purpose in man)* will completely revolutionize your prayer life and your expectations of God! If you have mixed faith with this Word of God your spiritual transformation is truly closer to you than you think. You must, Precious Hearts, continually seek God to receive from Him that measure of intimacy, trust and understanding that gains for you a clearer Revelation of God's ultimate purpose for your life! For it is then that *your potentials in Him will become totally unlimited! What you <u>Know </u>will completely change you* and *what you <u>become </u>will utterly change your world!* Consequently, it's entirely up to you to *learn so as to become something and someone that is the Father's potential for you;* something and someone *far greater than you have ever dreamed to be!* The undeniable truth is **"It's All in the Knowing!"**

A New Beginning

"Basking in the Sun of the Son"

➤◆◀━

An excerpt from my next book

Check this! While I sat here in my office musing on the immutability and the perfection of God and His handiwork, the Lord brought to my attention an article that I wrote last year after I visited my eldest son in West Palm Beach, Florida. This article is the first chapter in my next book.

I had decided that one morning before coming back home to Texas, I would go to the beach early in the morning to witness a sunrise over the Atlantic Ocean. I entitled the piece, ***"Basking in the Sun of the Son."*** Please enjoy this excerpt that expresses very clearly what I mean by **God's Perfection and His Immutable Workmanship** and **<u>know</u>** that the God of this episode in one man's life is also the God of your life!

"At some point, my focus was shifted to the waters of the Atlantic Ocean. As I gazed over the vast expanse of the ocean as far as my eyes could see, I was most singularly struck with an abiding sense of the endless scope and range of both the Presence and the Power of God. That the water exists and has existed

for untold eons stands as a testimony to the immutability of God's Presence and Power.

Slowly, as I enjoyed the salty spray on my cheeks, a thought began to take shape in my mind which was not a new thought at all but an idea revisited with a sharpness and a depth that I did not have until now! I have been conscious of the fact that since God first made the waters in the genesis of all things, He has never made any more water! I have known for some time that the same waters that the Father first made are the waters that we drink, bathe in and cook with today. This is true because there is very literally no place for water to go from this earth realm and no method for its complete and final removal. You see, water, whether used or not, simply changes form from liquid to steam to liquid to ice to liquid to steam ad infinitum. When I pondered this, I realized that this is not a new process. I dangled my feet, as I sat on this rock today, in the same waters that dinosaurs drank! And it was the same water that refreshed Adam and Eve in the Garden of Eden whose showers sprayed my feet! The same waters that caused the great flood in the days of Noah and the same water that John the Baptist baptized our Lord, Jesus Christ in almost two thousand years ago is the same water that cooled my feet and ankles in sparkles of silvery blue! How awesome is our God!"

The constancy and the faithful authenticity of the seascape included the sun in all of its brilliance; it included the beautiful azure water, the sandy beach, the birds and indeed all that was my world at that time, on that day. All that my awestruck eyes took in pronounced to me in a stentorian voice that the words God spoke in the beginning of time are still alive today! Experiencing these wonders, I knew with a depth of understanding that heretofore was beyond my ability to comprehend, that His Spoken Words are eternally influential! They will forever supply the Power and the Divine Directives that continue the life of His Divinely Spoken Ordination! For, His Words are "proceeding words!" (See Matt. 4:4)

*It was then that I felt, even as I saw, the light of the sun. As I experienced the sun in these two dimensions of feeling and sight, My Father gently reminded me that His infallible Word is the Power that **keeps the sun burning** and producing heat and light. Because, when God said, "Let there be light," He set in motion a law! Actually, what He literally said was, **"Let there be <u>light</u>, light,** light, light, light," to the end of time. Ever since God said, **"Let there be light,"** there has been light somewhere on earth! All of this demonstrates the faithfulness of God and solidifies, in my heart, the certainty and the surety of my future! Most assuredly my future is safe and intact for all of this life and **for as long as God lives!***

*When God saturated my mind and my spirit with these truths, He capped it off by **making me to <u>know</u> another truth!** He taught me that the aspect of God's love that causes His children to have faith in Him is "His Faithfulness!" Because He has always been Faithful—<u>we have faith in His Faithfulness (the strength of His Character that causes Him to never fail and never forget His children and His Promises to them!</u>)*

I sat on that rock that day in the city of West Palm Beach, Florida and wept. I wept for the promise that these truths gave me. I cried because of the tender touch of the Masters Hand on my heart. I wept because He condescended to one of such lowly estate. And I shed briny tears for the sense of relief and the discernment that even when I cannot understand the madness of my thoughts and my world—Understanding understands me! I cannot express to you with any modicum of accuracy the infusion of Power coupled with a working knowledge of my own insufficiency that was mine as He gave me a greater sense of purpose and a confidence in Himself as well as in myself.

ABOUT THE AUTHOR

Bishop J. A. Tolbert 1st has been married to his "Brown Sugar" for forty-seven years. They have raised four children and are blessed with ten grand children. Bishop Tolbert is the pastor of The Family Life Center Church where he has served for thirty-seven years. His greatest interest and his greatest love were his quest for Truth and all things that pertain to God. The Truths in his book were not bought cheaply. Rather, it was through the furnace of afflictions and in the school of "Knee-ology," that these Life changing realities were revealed by God!